D1415293

Match Wits with Baseball Experts

Wayne Stewart

Sterling Publishing Co., Inc.
New York

Dedication

To the "train" people: Al Shaffer, Brent Hutlock,
Cathy Burchell, Devalon Kyle, June Gregg, Ryan Coleman,
Steve Meggitt, and Susan Smith. Also to my wife Nancy
and our sons Scott and Sean.

Library of Congress Cataloging-in-Publication Data

Stewart, Wayne, 1951-
  Match wits with baseball experts : test your dugout savvy against the pros /
Wayne Stewart.
    p. cm.
  Includes index.
  ISBN 1-4027-2414-4
  1. Baseball--Problems, exercises, etc. 2. Baseball--Miscellanea. I. Title.

GV873S863 2006
796.357--dc22

                                                            2005020287

10 9 8 7 6 5 4 3 2 1

Published by Sterling Publishing Co., Inc.
387 Park Avenue South, New York, NY 10016
© 2006 by Wayne Stewart
Distributed in Canada by Sterling Publishing
c/o Canadian Manda Group, 165 Dufferin Street
Toronto, Ontario, Canada M6K 3H6
Distributed in the United Kingdom by GMC Distribution Services
Castle Place, 166 High Street, Lewes, East Sussex, England BN71XU
Distributed in Australia by Capricorn Link (Australia) Pty. Ltd.
P.O. Box 704, Windsor, NSW 2756, Australia

Sterling ISBN 13: 978-1-4027-2414-5
       ISBN 10: 1-4027-2414-4

CONTENTS

INTRODUCTION

In this book you will be asked to fill the shoes and/or spikes of baseball personnel from those in the field, such as managers and even umpires, to those manning the teams' front offices. In addition to your role-playing tasks, at times not only will your knowledge of baseball rules and strategy be put to the test, your general baseball I.Q. dealing with records, trivia, and even quotes will be under fire.

When it comes to the chapters on managerial moves, your decisions can sway the outcome of big league games. You'll be acting out real-life scenarios that legendary managers such as Walter Alston and Connie Mack had to cope with. More modern situations are covered too, with puzzlers faced by contemporary skippers such as Joe Torre, Dusty Baker, and Mike Hargrove. You can choose to play the percentages, as many managers do, or take an occasional risk and go against the "book." You may decide to call for a triple steal or even a suicide squeeze play. You may decide to yank a pitcher or let him tough it out despite a rising pitch count.

In another chapter, you will make decisions and transactions as if you were a big league team's general manager. Do you aggressively pursue a free agent who will deplete your team's bank account? Would you have tried to acquire a Carlos Beltran, an Ivan Rodriguez, or an Alex Rodriguez if you had the opportunity? You'll look back on some famous trades, too.

When it's your turn to be a major league umpire, you will have to prove you know the rules, and that's not always easy when presented with some wild real-life cases.

So your work is cut out for you. Read on and take the challenge!

Wayne Stewart

1
DEAN OF THE DUGOUT

In this leadoff chapter, you play the role of a big league manager, faced with actual situations from the major leagues. You must make managerial decisions; then read on to learn what happened in reality and/or to discover what experts have to say about the scenarios presented.

Interestingly, many experts have theorized over the years as to just how important the manager's role is when being translated into wins and losses. Some say a good manager can win an extra 5 to 10 games per year with his shrewd machinations, while a poor manager can drop an extra 5 to 10 with his inept handling of a team. Former manager Bob Boone seems to disagree somewhat. He once said in all modesty and sincerity, "Managers don't really win games, but they can lose plenty of them." He added, "If you're doing a quality job, you should be almost anonymous."

At any rate, here's your chance to pull the strings and make your moves.

1. STRANGE MOVE

Your name is Lloyd McClendon and you are the manager of the 2004 Pittsburgh Pirates. It's August 11 and you're facing the San Franciso Giants. The game is tied in the 10th inning and Barry Bonds, who once launched 73 home runs in a season, steps to the plate to get things started. In this situation, would you consider issuing a leadoff intentional walk? *The answer is on page 14.*

2. ANOTHER STRANGE MOVE

During a game in which Walt Alston managed the Brooklyn Dodgers, hard-hitting Roy Campanella was batting with the runner off first base representing the game-winning run. There were two outs and a 3-and-1 count, so Campy was expecting to see a good pitch to whack at. However, Alston had his third-base coach flash the "take" sign. Seconds later, quite dismayed at having just seen a juicy fastball go by for a called strike, taking him to a full count, Campanella dug in again, puzzled by the decision to take a pitch. What was Alston's logic behind this seemingly strange maneuver? If you were running the Dodgers, would you have made that call? *The answer is on page 14.*

3. BACK TO BONDS

The San Francisco Giants took on Randy Johnson and his Arizona Diamondbacks on July 9, 2004. With San Francisco runners on first and second in the bottom of the fifth, the game, then tied at three apiece, had reached a crucial moment. A classic confrontation arose: Johnson with his 4,000-plus strikeouts versus the much-feared Bonds in a lefty-on-lefty match-up featuring future Hall of Famers. Normally Johnson would not walk a batter in this situation, but would you direct him to give four wide ones to Bonds? *The answer is on page 15.*

4. PLAYING IT BY THE BOOK

In baseball jargon, playing it "by the book" refers to managerial decisions that make the most sense percentage-wise, conforming totally to analytical scouting reports and computer printouts. Sometimes a manager will play it by the book and other times he'll make decisions based more on his heart and gut instinct.

Imagine you are Phil Garner when he led the Milwaukee Brewers back in 1999. Southpaw Jesse Orosco, an outstanding reliever, is in your bullpen anxiously waiting to enter the game, but a pack of right-handed hitters are due up. Would you consider making the call to Orosco anyway?

The answer is on page 15.

5. GOING AGAINST CONVENTIONAL THINKING

Yet another example of going against the book took place during the 2004 American League Championship Series. Joe Torre, the New York Yankees skipper, told the press later that when his team played the Boston Red Sox in cozy Fenway Park, its dimensions caused him to sometimes alter his thinking process regarding stolen base attempts with runners in scoring position. How could the stadium's size and configuration influence his strategy in this regard?

The answer is on page 16.

6. THROW THE BOOK AWAY?

During the 1999 season, Tony Muser, the manager of the Kansas City Royals was faced with a dilemma with his team playing the Texas Rangers. The Rangers had a runner on second courtesy of a sacrifice bunt, and Rusty Greer coming to the plate. He would be followed by Juan Gonzalez, a master at knocking in runs. First base was open, but the Royals needed a double play. Did Muser elect to pitch to Greer, or did he walk him to set up a double play? Had this been your call, what would you have done?

The answer is on page 16.

7. CALL TO THE BULLPEN?

In July 1999, Detroit Tigers manager Larry Parrish said, "We've been using the [computer and scouting] matchups of how some guys do against our pitchers to help decide which reliever to bring in, and we've been beat a couple times by pitchers who never gave up a hit to this guy—but you bring him in to pitch and, boom, base hit and game's over."

With that string of bad luck against Parrish, what did he do when his Tigers squared off against the Cincinnati Reds in a key spot with the dangerous Greg Vaughn at the plate? The situation was this: Vaughn, who wound up the season with 45 homers, was a good candidate to hurt Detroit with his stick or, on the other hand, to strike out—he ended the year with a staggering 137 whiffs.

Parrish had Willie Blair up in the bullpen, but, as Parrish recalled, "At the time, he was like 8-for-12 off Willie with a couple of homers." Did Parrish play it the conventional way, relying on printouts, and go to the pen for a pitcher who had a history of doing well versus Vaughn, or did he elect to chance it with Blair?

The answer is on page 16.

8. HARGROVE TOOK A CHANCE

Then there was an incident that took place on August 18, 1999. The Cleveland Indians were playing the Rangers and the blazing hot Rafael Palmeiro came to the plate in the seventh inning. The score was tied at one run each, with Rangers dancing off second and third. An obvious call would be to order an intentional walk from right-handed pitcher Charles Nagy to the left-handed hitting Palmeiro. Was this another situation where the manager Mike Hargrove didn't make the "normal" move?

The answer is on page 17.

9. PLAYING THE LEFTY-LEFTY PERCENTAGES

It's June 28, 2005, and the Los Angeles Angels and Texas Rangers, the two top dogs in the American League West Division, are battling in an early showdown. Knotted at one run apiece and entering the 11th inning, the Angels load the bases with star outfielder Garret Anderson coming to the plate. If you were in the trembling spikes of Texas manager Bucky Showalter, do you go to the pen to bring a southpaw into the game to face the left-handed hitting Anderson?   *The answer is on page 17.*

10. CHECK AND DOUBLE-CHECK

This time you play the role of Buddy Bell, managing the Kansas City Royals in 2005 after replacing Tony Pena. On July 1, you turn in your lineup card to the umpires prior to the game's first pitch against the visiting Angels. In the bottom of the first inning, David DeJesus gets your Royals off to a fine start by banging a single. That brings Angel Berroa to the plate.

But wait—the umpires huddle and point out that, according to the card presented to them, Berroa is hitting out of order; Berroa is supposed to hit leadoff and DeJesus is penciled in as the number two man in the batting order.

Two questions: When the umps rule DeJesus must abandon his berth on first and bat again with an automatic out being declared on Berroa's spot in the lineup, do you protest this call, or are they correct? Secondly, who is responsible for the botched lineup card—one of your coaches or yourself?   *The answer is on page 17.*

11. AN OLDER MOVE

In Game 4 of the 1947 World Series between the Yankees and the Dodgers, New York hurler Bill Bevins was flirting with history, carrying a no-hitter into the ninth inning. With one out and nursing a one-run lead, Bevins walked Brooklyn's Carl Furillo and then got the next batter on a pop-up. Al Gionfriddo swiped second as a pinch runner, putting the tying run in scoring position.

At that point pinch hitter Pete Reiser, a pretty dangerous stick coming off a .309 season, was announced. Would it make sense to give him a free pass and work to the next hitter? *The answer is on page 18.*

12. THE NAME OF THE GAME

Easy one: What is, by far, the most important aspect of baseball, that is to say, if a team is strong in this department, it will usually win more than its share of contests? Is it: A) a solid bench to spell your regulars; B) pitching in general; C) a closer out of the bullpen; D) one or more sluggers in the middle of the lineup; or E) great gloves up the middle?

The answer is on page 18.

13. STEAL SIGNS?

Is it legal within the rules of the game to steal signs from your opponents? If so, how would a manager use the intelligence his espionage team discovered?

The answer is on page 19.

14. WORLD SERIES CRUNCH TIME

Imagine it's the Fall Classic of 1962 and your hand is on the rudder of the Yankees (in reality, their manager was Ralph Houk). When the last of the ninth was finally reached in the Series finale, nerves were frayed and fingernails had long been chewed away. Your Yanks are nursing a 1–0 lead when the Giants rallied and had Matty Alou on third and Willie Mays leading off second, representing the possible Series-winning run. To make matters worse, the monstrous Willie McCovey was in the batter's box with the solid hitting Orlando Cepeda due next.

What do you do now? Walk McCovey, since his run means nothing, realizing, though, that the move would fill the bases and the peril of a run-scoring walk to Cepeda was palpable? Pitch to McCovey with righty Ralph Terry who is in the middle of twirling a four-hit shutout? Go to the bullpen to bring in a lefty to put out the McCovey fire?

The answer is on page 20.

15. MARATHON PITCHER

Here's a hypothetical situation. Randy Johnson is spinning a gem, with a two-hitter through seven innings. He's thrown an economical 98 pitches so far. If he manages to keep that pace up of around 14 pitches or so per inning, how long would you, playing the role of Johnson's manager Joe Torre, stick with him?

The answer is on page 20.

16. MARATHON, PART II

Let's change things up a bit. Say your starter gets bombed in the first inning so you replace him after a mere two outs have been recorded, with a rubber-armed long relief man. Imagine that you come in with a guy like Tim Wakefield, normally a starter, but a guy who throws the knuckleball, which would allow him to work countless innings without tiring. Just how long would you use him?

The answer is on page 20

17. DISCIPLINARY MATTERS

Part of a manager's job is that of a disciplinarian. During a Cleveland Indians game on September 23, 1999, Manny Ramirez, known for his stick but not for his glove, loafed while in pursuit of a foul fly ball that landed near the left field foul line. Tribe manager Mike Hargrove instantly knew that if Ramirez had hustled, he could have made the catch to retire a Tigers batter.

What action did Hargrove take?: A) He immediately yanked him from the contest; B) he waited for the inning to end, and then reprimanded Ramirez on the bench; C) he scolded him in private the next day; or D) he fined him.

The answer is on page 20.

18. GIVE HIM THE HOOK?

Nowadays, when a manager visits a pitcher on the mound during a tense moment, he has usually made up his mind to pull the pitcher. Put yourself in the place of Oakland A's manager Ken Macha during a 2004 contest. You've bolted out of the dugout, approached your starter, Mark Mulder, and now he's telling you he feels fine and wants to stay in the game. Do you go with your pitcher's testimony, or is it dangerous to set a precedence by allowing a player to talk you out of making a move?

The answer is on page 21.

19. SWING AWAY?

During an Indians game on June 17, 2001, Charlie Manuel was running the club and his pitcher, rookie C.C. Sabathia, was due up at the plate in an interleague game in Pittsburgh. With the bases loaded and one out, the Indians and Pirates were deadlocked at 0–0 in the fifth inning. As an American League pitcher, Sabathia seldom had the chance to swing a bat; he had only one big league at bat under his belt. In such a situation, would you pinch hit for him or allow him to hack away?

The answer is on page 21.

20. SWING AWAY, PART II

Having decided to stick with Sabathia, what did Manuel order when the count ran 3–1 to him while facing Pirates pitcher Todd Ritchie? Did he give him the take sign or allow him to use his own judgment on the next delivery? *The answer is on page 21.*

21. C.C. ONE MORE TIME

On May 21, 2005, Sabathia, then hitting .273 over 22 lifetime at-bats, must have felt vindicated when he launched a game-winning, two-run homer to dead centerfield over the head of Ken Griffey, Jr. in a 5–3 win over the Cincinnati Reds. Three frames later, in the seventh, after he had thrown 102 pitches, he was due to lead off the inning. Manager Eric Wedge had a decision to make this time: Stick with him and let him bat or replace him with a pinch hitter. Actually, he could have let Sabathia bat, seen the results, and then decided if he wanted to keep him on the mound. Say Sabathia hit a double. With Sabathia in scoring position, representing an important insurance run, Wedge could have then pinch run for the lumbering Sabathia. What would you do? *The answer is on page 21.*

1. In theory, you absolutely never put a leadoff runner on in any inning. They say leadoff walks come around to score about 40 to 50 percent of the time, so to purposely give a pass to a batter is highly risky. Additionally, most skippers won't intentionally put the potential tying run on base, let alone the possible winning run. After all, what upside would there be to such moves?

However, that's exactly what McClendon instructed his team to do. McClendon's logic was simple: If the Pirates pitcher slipped and made one mistake, the torrid Bonds could easily homer and the Pirates would more than likely lose. However, working around Bonds allowed his staff to battle lesser hitters, taking their chances with them. Even though the Giants loaded the bases that frame, they failed to score and the Pirates went on to win, 8–6. The odd, brazen McClendon move worked.

2. A look at what happened on the Campanella play. With a payoff pitch due, the runner from first took off while the pitcher, not wanting to issue a walk that would move the potential game-winning runner into scoring position, knew he had to throw a strike. In such situations pitchers almost always serve up a fastball. Alston knew all this when he made his decision, and, sure enough, Campy got his fastball, laced a long single to the outfield, and the Dodgers won the contest. If the pitcher had gotten cute and thrown a pitch off the plate, Campanella would simply have taken a free stroll to first.

Alston also knew that if Campanella had singled on the earlier 3–1 count, the runner off first would not have had the advantage of running on the pitch and would have wound up at third. The only danger of taking a 3–1 pitch was that Campy might whiff on the full count, but Alston was confident his hitter would see a good pitch to swing at.

3. Johnson did walk Bonds even though that loaded the bases and shoved two men into scoring position to make a tight spot in a close game even tighter. The next batter was Edgardo Alfonzo, who hit a line drive to Luis Gonzalez in left field, so the ploy worked. But wait. Gonzalez dropped the ball for a costly error. Furthermore, after center fielder Steve Finley, backing up the play, got to the ball, his throw back to shortstop Alex Cintron was low and skimmed off the grass. All three runners scored, busting the game wide open and the Giants waltzed to an 8–3 win.

Bonds, by the way, is one of only three men to have been given an intentional walk with the bases loaded. The others were Nap Lajoie in 1901 and Bill Nicholson in 1944.

4. Often young, insecure managers will "cover themselves" by playing it safe and by utterly and completely going by the book. Nevertheless, established skippers such as Phil Garner have proven unafraid to take chances. Garner recalled how he'd go against the book with Jessie Orosco. "I'd bring him in to face a left-hander knowing that all the managers would bring in right-handers," said Garner, pointing out the opposing managers were, by making such a move, playing it 100 percent by the book.

However, said Garner, "My book was the opposite with Jesse, and it worked with him. Jesse had much better numbers against right-handers. I can't tell you the number of times Jesse would get us a ground ball double play against right-handers."

5. Normally a team never tries to swipe third base with two outs since, with the runner at second already in scoring position he is almost certain to cross home plate on a two-out hit, there is little to be gained in taking the chance of being gunned down at third. Still, explained Torre, "It's not necessarily a bad play to try to steal third here [Fenway Park] with two outs because it's so tough to score with a single to left field from second because it's so shallow."

★

6. Muser recalls, "We needed a double play, and even though Gonzalez is leading the world in RBI, really, the only way out of the jam was a ground ball double play. So we walked Greer to set up our double play and we got our ground ball, but Gonzalez hit it in the seam between third and short, and we got beat.

"Everybody says, 'Well, why do you walk Greer to pitch to the big RBI guy?' And I said, 'Because it's the only way out of this jam.' I had confidence that we could get a ground ball with a ground ball pitcher on the mound.

"They [the media] thought I was stupid, but Johnny gave us an out by bunting. So we've got one out, now we're only two away from getting out of the jam. So, I will pitch into the meat of the order. I think once in awhile you have to do that; you can't pitch around people all the time."

★

7. Parrish played a hunch, and was delighted that "against Cincinnati, [our bad luck] went the other way. Vaughn was having trouble with the curve ball and even though he has hit Blair [well in the past], Blair should be a good match-up for him if he throws his breaking ball, so we brought Willie in and Willie struck him out."

8. Yes. The Tribe pitched to him, and the splendid first baseman made them pay. He drilled an 0–1 pitch, pulling it to right field for a three-run home run. For all intentions, the game was over.

Manager Mike Hargrove explained his strategy to *The Plain Dealer*. He said the plan was to pitch around Palmeiro, but Nagy made a mistake, offering a pitch that was too tempting, way too fat.

Hargrove said, "You pitch around guys all the time in the big leagues. It's an unintentional intentional walk. If we had fallen behind him, we would have walked him. There are times when you go against the book. I get hammered here a lot for going too much by the book. This time I went against the book, but it didn't work out." Such is the life of big league skippers.

9. Normally, that's the way to play this scenario out. Further, that's how Showalter handled it. However, when Anderson ripped a grand slam off the sidearming Brian Shouse, all was lost for Texas that day. Although Shouse had held Anderson hitless in their previous six encounters, Anderson actually was a .615 hitter versus lefty relievers on the year based on his eight hits, including two homers, in 13 at-bats.

10. The umpires were absolutely correct in their call and Berroa won't bat until the next time through the order. So, not only can't you protest the ruling, you have no one to blame but yourself for the faux pas. These kinds of mistakes shouldn't happen at the big league level, but, from time to time, they do.

Bell confessed, "Checking the lineup card doesn't take much energy to do. The bottom line is, I didn't double-check the official lineup card with the card on the [dugout] wall. It's totally, totally my responsibility. It was inexcusable and irresponsible."

11. Walking him to place the potential winning run aboard seems foolhardy, but that's what Yankee skipper Bucky Harris did. The results were disastrous: The Dodgers countered with yet another pinch-hitter, Cookie Lavagetto, who promptly drilled a double to right, breaking up the no-hitter while clinching a 3–2 Brooklyn victory.

12. While every one of the multiple choices is important, the answer is B—pitching plain and simple. Over the years experts have said that pitching is as high as 90 percent of the key to winning. In 2004 Larry Bowa, then manager of the Phillies, told *Philadelphia Inquirer* writer Todd Zolecki, "The name of the game is pitching . . . If you want to look at box scores, all you have to do is look at the starting pitching on both teams. That's what it's all about. You get your starting pitcher to go seven innings, you get into your bullpen and you use your set-up guy and closer. That's how the game is supposed to be played."

In 1969 the upstart New York Mets, a pathetic franchise up to that point, startled the baseball world by transforming themselves into the "Amazin' Mets," World Series winners. Early in the year skeptics said the team's sticks were too weak for the team to go very far, pointing out that they had no big name hitters on their roster. Other than Cleon Jones, no starter topped the .280 plateau, and Tommie Agee, their top "slugger," hit only 26 homers with a feeble team-leading 76 RBI. What they did have, though, was outstanding pitching led by Tom Seaver, who led the league in wins with 25, and 17-game winner Jerry Koosman.

Most recently, the Atlanta Braves won an unprecedented 13 consecutive division titles. They did so with a pitching staff that placed either first or second in the entire majors for team ERA in an eye-popping 12 of those 13 magnificent seasons.

13. Stealing signs has been going on at the major league level for decades upon decades. If a team isn't clever enough to disguise its signals, or if the enemy is sharp enough to decipher those signs, then a "spying" manager certainly will take advantage of the data.

One of the best in the business at stealing signs was Joe Nossek, with over 30 years' total experience as a player, minor league manager, and big league coach. While working under Milwaukee manager Del Crandall, Nossek frequently fed information that Crandall acted upon. For example, if Nossek's espionage had detected the steal sign, Crandall would call for a pitch out, giving his catcher a huge edge in trying to nail the runner.

Nossek added a secondary advantage to sign stealing. "I've been able to get a reputation for doing that, and it's served me well because even if you're not stealing anything, the psychological advantage may inhibit the other team at times."

Nossek also spoke about a cat and mouse game that took place when the Brewers met Texas, then under manager Billy Martin. "We had their signs, so I turned to Crandall and said, 'Billy's got the squeeze on.' So Del whistled to the catcher for a pitchout. Billy saw this and promptly took the squeeze off."

Since Nossek also noticed Martin make that counter-move, the Brewers canceled the pitchout, and that prompt-ed Martin to get "his third base coach's attention," to put the squeeze play on once more. Not to be outdone, Crandall called for the pitchout yet again.

Nossek said this went back and forth about three times. "Finally, Billy kept it on and we put the pitchout back on and got the runner at the plate. That was one of the few times we got the upper hand on Billy; he was good. He was smart so it was fun to go against him," said Nossek of the diamond's version of a multilayered chess game.

14. Houk has faith in Terry and allowed him to go right at McCovey. The slugger got a pitch to his liking and positively starched it, but the resulting fierce line drive headed directly towards and into the glove of second baseman Bobby Richardson. Game over. It was a "Whew!" moment for Houk and his Yankees to be sure, but they had boldly notched another world championship.

15. The answer is pretty much up to you with input from Johnson on how he feels. Typically nowadays, valuable starters don't toil for more than say 130 pitches, with pitch counts scrutinized under microscope-like attention.

16. Assuming you don't need him to make a start soon, Wakefield could easily give you as many innings as you might expect out of one of his starts. For the sake of argument, and to illustrate a point, let's just say he'd kill ten innings.

Now a real life situation: On June 17, 1915, certainly in a different era, the Cubs' George "Zip" Zabel was summoned from the bullpen with two outs in the first and he proceeded to pitch endless innings. Eventually, he won a 4–3 decision after 19 frames, the longest relief stint in major league history. It is highly unlikely any man will ever again be called upon so long.

17. All of the multiple choices make sense, but in this case Hargrove pulled him from the game. The next day, a seemingly contrite Ramirez pounded a grand slam and a three-run shot, good for a career-high eight ribbies in an 18–4 thrashing of Toronto.

18. Somewhat surprisely, Macha said that when he spoke with Mulder he would get the truth out of him (unlike many pitchers who refuse to admit they're floundering). "I trust Mark 1,000 percent," said Macha.

19. Manuel let him take his cuts and later explained with a grin, "C.C. is a good hitter. Go ask him. He'll tell you he's a good hitter." Sabathia commented that he was pretty good in high school with a bat in his hands. "If you don't hit .400 in high school, you're not doing much. But that was two years ago. Now I'm facing a 94 mph fastball."

20. Although he took some heat for his call, Manuel let him hit away. Unfortunately for the Indians, Sabathia hit the ball sharply on the ground to third base for the start of an around-the-horn double play to end the inning and to kill the only real scoring opportunity on the night; the Pirates prevailed, 1–0.

Sabathia commented that he wasn't given a take sign, then added, "I mean, I don't know the signs, but I'm sure if they wanted me not to swing, Joel Skinner [third base coach] would have yelled to me."

21. Wedge, frustrated with this team's lethargic offense around that time of the seaon, let his starting pitcher bat. After he grounded out, Wedge gave him the night off and went to the bullpen. "I didn't want to use another player," explained Wedge of his unusual move, "and C.C. had certainly hit the guy well in his previous at bat. There was no harm in letting him have another chance."

2

YOU'RE THE "MAN IN BLACK"

U mpires were once nicknamed the "men in black" when their uniforms were still traditionally that color. Fashion aside, it's your turn to "witness" situations and make a split-second call.

1. GROUND RULE

Moises Alou was playing left field in Wrigley Field for the Cubs. Houston's Adam Everett ripped a ball which deflected off Alou's glove and nestled in the ivy on the wall. Alou hoisted his arms giving the usual signal to umpires that a ball was lost, not in play. What ruling did the umps make? *The answer is on page 31.*

2. INFIELD FLY SITUATION

When Orlando Gomez was Tampa Bay's bullpen coach, he discussed a bizarre play he once saw involving the infield fly rule in a bases loaded situation. The batter lofted a high fly to the infield and was, of course, by the nature of the rule, declared out. However, the ball got lost in the sun, fell to the dirt, and skipped a short distance away from the nearest fielder. The runner off third took off for home, an ensuing throw came home also, but "the catcher forgot to tag the guy; he forced the runner by tagging home plate instead of the runner."

  In this situation would you call a double play, render the ball dead and send the runner back to third, allow the run to score, or scratch your head in puzzlement?

The answer is on page 31.

3. GIVE HIM THE THUMB

Can an umpire eject a batter from a game during an intentional walk? *The answer is on page 32.*

4. YOU'RE BLIND, UMP

An organist playing at a minor league park in 1993 decided to play "Three Blind Mice" as that day's umpires took to the field just prior to the game. Witty, perhaps, but it was offensive to the umpiring crew.

One year prior to that, Jerry Burkot, the public address announcer for another minor league team, the Greensboro Hornets, also ruffled some egos. After what he felt was a questionable third strike call, he piped the theme song from "The Twilight Zone" over the sound system. Earlier he had been warned not to play that tune to mock the umps, but he couldn't resist.

Do umpires have the right to eject teams' personnel such as the men mentioned, or do their "veto" powers of thumbing someone apply only to players, managers, and coaches? *The answer is on page 32.*

5. FINAL EJECTION SCENARIO

The Morning Journal featured an odd tale that took place when Detroit hosted Cleveland on May 2, 1995, in a contest being umpired by a crew of replacements who were hired due to a labor dispute involving big league umps. Positive that the pitch he delivered to Tigers outfielder Bobby Higginson was a strike, Dennis Martinez stormed off the mound. He confronted home plate umpire Gus Klein, holding the ball directly over the middle of home plate, indicating where the pitch had traveled. Is this case of "showing up the umpire" enough to get Martinez tossed? *The answer is on page 32.*

6. SWITCH PITCH

Switch-hitters are common in professional baseball, but pitchers who have the skill to throw with both arms are as rare as sweet talk between Yankees and Red Sox.

During his high school days Paul Richards once won the first game of a doubleheader while throwing righty then came back to win the nightcap while firing the ball lefty. In a minor league contest Richards, normally a right-hander, was on the mound when a pinch-hitter strolled to the plate. It was Charlie Wilson, a switch hitter.

Question: As an umpire, what would you do in this situation? Wilson took his position to bat left-handed against Richards, but when he did so Richards simply took the glove off his left hand, switched the ball to that hand, and was prepared to go at Wilson lefty-on-lefty, an advantage for the pitcher. Can Wilson now turn around and decide he's going to bat righty after all? Could Richards then change his mind again? What's your call?

The answer is on page 33.

7. HOW MANY OUTS?

It doesn't happen often, but players are humans and do forget the number of outs sometimes. In 1979, Joe Ferguson was batting for the Dodgers against the Pittsburgh Pirates with the bases loaded and a payoff pitch on the way. Lee Lacy, the runner off third, saw what he believed was strike three, but was actually ball four. Unaware, Lacy trudged toward the dugout.

Confusion set in when Pirates catcher Manny Sanguillen also thought the inning was over! He removed the ball from his mitt and rolled it toward the mound for the start of the next inning. At that point Jim Wynn, the runner from second base, sprinted around third and crossed home plate. Lacy finally snapped out of his confusion and streaked across the plate, too. After unraveling the mess, the umpires made a ruling—what was it?

The answer is on page 33.

8. TIME OUT NEEDED!

A game on August 29, 1992, featured a huge mental mistake. Pitcher Charlie Leibrandt racked up his 1,000th career strikeout. Wishing to save the souvenir ball, he gently bowled it into his team's dugout. Big problem—he had failed to call a time out. Is the ball alive? Could the only base runner at the time, Ricky Jordan, advance?

The answer is on page 33.

9. INTERFERENCE VERSUS OBSTRUCTION

On August 6, 2004, Carl Crawford of the host Tampa Bay Devil Rays was on third base with the bases loaded and one out in the 10th inning of a 1–1 contest. Tino Martinez raised a fly ball to left field causing Crawford to head back toward third in order to tag up. Seattle's shortstop, Jose Lopez, purposely placed himself in a position to block Crawford's view of the catch by outfielder Raul Ibanez, hoping Lopez wouldn't get a good jump in his effort to score. What ruling would you make here? *The answer is on page 34.*

10. REVERSAL

On July 28, 2004, Justin Morneau of the Minnesota Twins hit a long drive that was ruled a homer by umpire Ed Montague. Chicago White Sox manager Carlos Guillen and his left fielder Carlos Lee protested the call. Replays revealed that the ball had hit the top of the fence and had ricocheted back onto the field. Can the umpiring crew reverse such a call? *The answer is on page 34.*

11. TOUCH 'EM ALL

It was the bottom of the 15th inning of the fifth game of the 1999 National League Championship Series. The bases were full of Mets and Atlanta's rookie pitcher Kevin McGlinchy had his work cut out, facing veteran Robin Ventura in a 3–3 tie.

Ventura won the confrontation, belting a grand slam, a dramatic blow, on the 482nd pitch of the five hour and 46-minute game. Hold on, though. Ventura touched first base just moments before a wild and jubilant celebration broke out. Mobbed by teammates, he never bothered to run around the base paths. What's your call here?

The answer is on page 34.

12. SIMILAR PLAY

When Chris Chambliss hit the pennant-winning, ninth-inning walk-off homer for the Yankees versus Kansas City in the 1976 American League Championship Series, things were a bit different. He glided around the bases until a throng of fans engulfed him at home plate. It was unclear if he had touched the plate or not.

As a matter of fact, about an hour after the game he returned to the field to step on home plate, just in case he had missed it. Alan Robinson of the AP quoted Chambliss as saying, "Home plate was gone. Somebody had already taken it. There were no umps there, either." In theory, could Kansas City have appealed the play later?

The answer is on page 34.

13. IT USUALLY PAYS TO STEAL

Roger Cedeno stole third base for the Mets on a play in which home plate ump Sam Holbrook got in the way of Yankees catcher Jorge Posada, who was trying to unleash a throw. Is it Posada's responsibility to get into a position to get his throw off, or is the umpire at fault here?

The answer is on page 35.

14. GOING AGAINST THE GRAIN

Is there anything in the rule book that prohibits a switch-hitter who is, say, facing a left-handed pitcher, from batting lefty? Obviously, this would be poor strategy on the surface of things, but if you were the umpire would you allow this?   *The answer is on page 35.*

15. RUNNER AND BALL MEET

A base runner off first base is headed toward second on a grounder. Suddenly, the ball strikes him on an erratic hop. As the ump, what ruling do you make?

The answer is on page 36.

16. STAYING INSIDE THE LINES

Let's say Craig Biggio of the Houston Astros is dashing down the line, trying to beat out a grounder. He's safe on a photo finish at first, but he did not stay inside the "lane," the restraining path that's delineated by chalk near the first-base bag. In running outside that lane, he made contact with the first baseman. Is the contact incidental or is Biggio violating a rule?

The answer is on page 36.

17. WILD TIMES

During the fourth game of the American League Championship Series of 1999, things got rather wild. In the bottom of the ninth, frustrated Boston Red Sox fans threw bottles on the field, resulting in an eight-minute delay. New York Yankees players, at risk, were hustled off the field. Yankees second baseman Chuck Knoblauch commented, "That's not a safe situation. You have to have eyes all over the place." Can an umpire in this situation stop the game entirely?

The answer is on page 36.

18. WRONG CALL

The Houston Astros met the St. Louis Cardinals on April 24, 2005, and, in the sixth inning, loaded the bases to set up a bizarre event. Cards third baseman Scott Rolen made a backhanded stab on a short hop line drive off the bat of Craig Biggio. Rolen stabbed the bag with his spikes for a force out and rifled the ball across the infield to nab Biggio. Then, when first baseman Albert Pujols applied a tag to Willy Taveras, who was still standing on the bag at first, the ump called Taveras out for the completion of a triple play. Just one problem, though, it isn't a triple killing—why not?

The answer is on page 36.

19. EJECTION TIME FOR THE EARL OF BALTIMORE

Baltimore manager Earl Weaver was notorious for his volatile temper and for the numerous ejections that resulted from his ire. One day veteran umpire Tom Haller spotted Weaver smoking a cigarette in the dugout during a game; he immediately gave Weaver the boot.

The next day the impish Weaver strolled to home plate to present his lineup card to the umpiring crew prior to the game. Haller once more spotted a cigarette in Weaver's mouth and ejected him again. Instead of getting upset, Weaver grinned and displayed his candy cigarette to Haller. Not amused, Haller kicked him out of the game before a single pitch was thrown. Is this a legitimate call?

The answer is on page 37.

20. POST GAME BLUES

It's May 7, 1997, and umpire Dale Ford's out call on Scott Brosius has just ended a 1–0 nailbiter. Brosius, upset that he was out at the plate and that his Oakland A's lost on that close call, fired his helmet to the turf and screamed at Ford. When A's manager Art Howe unleashed another tirade against Ford, he, too, was kicked out.

But can a man get kicked out of a game that's over?

The answer is on page 37.

21. GUARANTEED NIGHT OFF

One veteran ump said there are three things he would not permit a manager, coach, or player to do. Violating these three rules meant instant ejection. Can you name two?

The answer is on page 37.

22. FAUX PAS

Astrologists would love the wacky events of September 9, 1999, which numerically works out to 9–9–99. The San Diego Padres played host to the Montreal Expos in a game they'd go on to win, 10–3. In the seventh inning, the stars were aligned in favor of the Padres for awhile. Reggie Sanders of the Padres struck out for the inning's third out, but nobody—not the umps, the Padres, or the Expos realized the inning was over. That brought Phil Nevin to the plate. He worked the count to 2 and 1 against Ted Lilly before a member of the Expos called the mistake to the attention of home plate ump Jerry Layne. What happens next?

The answer is on page 37.

23. THE CALL TO THE PEN

Freddy Garcia was on the mound for Ozzie Guillen's Chicago White Sox on July 22, 2004, facing the Indians. He was coasting along into the eighth inning with nine strikeouts racked up. However, when he walked leadoff hitter Omar Vizquel, Guillen, who had a lefty and a righty warming up in the bullpen, felt it was time to make a change. As Guillen marched to the mound to lift Garcia, he knew he wanted southpaw Damaso Marte to enter the game. However, he inadvertently motioned with his right hand to indicate he wanted rightly reliever Cliff Politte to replace Garcia. If you were the umpire, what would you do here?

The answer is on page 37.

24. HE THREW HIS WHAT?!

A strange, seldom-called rule came into play during a Los Angeles versus Arizona contest on May 28, 2005. Dodgers reliever, hard-throwing Duaner Sanchez faced Luis Terrero, who hit a soft line drive that was headed back through the box. At first Sanchez leaped for the ball as if to stab it with his glove in the orthodox manner, but when he realized the ball was too high to haul in, he quickly removed his mitt from his left hand and tossed it right-handed at the ball. Further, he hit the ball in flight! He then scrambled over toward the earthbound ball, recovered it, and shoveled it to first base, a bit late to retire Terrero. If you had been the umpire that day, what would your ruling have been on this offbeat play?

The answer is on page 38.

25. INFIELD FLY PUZZLE

A strange play occurred on September 3, 2004 in Tampa. Detriot's Craig Monroe doubled to start an inning and Carlos Pena followed, drawing a walk. Marcus Thames then popped one up to Devil Rays shortstop Julio Lugo, who apparently lost the ball in the domed roof. The ball fell harmlessly to the ground. Monroe took off for third and Pena moved to second but not before a Tampa fielder stepped on third base. What's the correct call to clarify this mess? *The answer is on page 38.*

26. SCORER'S DECISION

Put away your umpire's equipment for this final quiz and pretend you're the scorer at a baseball game. How would you rule this play? On June 27, 2005, Boston's Trot Nixon, in a play similar to one made famous by Jose Canseco, was crestfallen when a long drive off the bat of Cleveland's Grady Sizemore deflected off his glove and into the stands, just a few yards to the left of the 380' marker in right field. Nixon had backpedaled on the ball, got turned around a bit, and although he did get the tip of his mitt on the ball, it set to rest in the visitor's bullpen. That turned a 4–0 Cleveland lead into a 6–0 cushion in the seventh inning.

Incidentally, in Canseco's more embarrassing incident, also against the Indians, the fly ball hit off his head and over the wall! Meanwhile, is Nixon charged with an error or do you award a homer to Sizemore?

The answer is on page 38.

★ CHAPTER 2 ANSWERS ★

1. Normally when a ball is, say, lodged under a fence or hidden among vines, the batter is awarded a ground rule double. However, once Alou touched the ball, that ground rule is not in effect. Everett was free to circle the bases, which he did. The scorer ruled the play a double and a two-base error. After the game Alou meekly told the gathered media, "I didn't know the rule." He added jokingly, "That's why I can't manage when I retire."

★

2. Orlando Gomez said, "There's no force, you have to tag the guy to make the double play." Therefore, since the rule states the ball is live and runners can advance at their own risk, the run stands. The force play no longer existed once the batter was automatically ruled out in this infield fly scenario.

3. An umpire can kick a player out of a game at any time, but it's hard to imagine a batter who is about to get a free pass to first being angry enough to do anything to precipitate an ejection.

Yet it has happened. Terry Francona, who would go on to manage the 2004 Red Sox to the world's championship, once was tossed from a game immediately after drawing an intentional walk. With bad blood already existing between him and home plate ump Ken Kaiser, Francona fumed when Kaiser muttered, "Can you believe they're intentionally walking you?" Having been insulted, Francona snapped, and accused the umpire of not hustling on an earlier play. Moments later, after ball four had been lobbed, Kaiser gave him the thumb in an odd baseball moment.

4. In both cases, the offending parties were kicked out of the game. In Burkot's instance, he was escorted out of the building on orders from an umpire. Sheriff's deputies took him away in handcuffs according to reports.

5. Normally, yes. Umps will allow a player to grumble about a call, but once a player shows an entire stadium that he is questioning the umpire's authority, such behavior results in the ol' heave-ho.

In this circumstance, with an umpire who was perhaps intimidated by his surroundings, he let the Martinez tirade pass. Tigers manager Sparky Anderson observed, "In 26 years I've never seen a pitcher go to the plate and hold the ball over the plate. The umpire said he should have thrown him out of the game, but by the time he realized it, it was too late."

Martinez was also responsible for another rarity that day— he apologized to Klein and confided that he "should have thrown me out. He just smiled." Martinez also pointed out that if a "real" umpire had been working the game "I'd be back in Cleveland now. But if we had a real ump, he wouldn't have missed the call."

6. The rule now states that the batter gets the final say in determining the match-up. It also indicates a pitcher can change hands on every pitch if he desires to do so. He is required to make his decision concerning which arm to use before stepping on the mound so the batter can then choose which batter's box he wants to enter.

However, in the Wilson vs. Richards case, records show Richards played it coy. He put both of his feet on the rubber, hid the ball behind his back, cradling it with both hands, and waited for Wilson to make his final decision as to which way he'd hit. At that point, Richards began his delivery throwing with the arm that gave him an edge over Wilson. Nevertheless, the result wound up in Wilson's favor when, quite anticlimactically, Richards walked him.

7. The pitch had been called ball four so the walk was issued to Ferguson. More important, since the ball was live, Lacy's run counted, but Wynn was ruled out for passing a runner and the inning of insanity was finally over.

In a not-as-messy situation from August 4, 1996, White Sox catcher Robert Machado rolled the ball back to the mound after a strikeout. He and pitcher Jim Parque were certain they had retired the side and began to leave the field. On the other hand, the alert Fred McGriff of Tampa Bay realized there were only two men out and scored all the way from second.

★

8. With no time out, the ball was alive, naturally. The runner advanced to second on this blunder.

9. Lopez is guilty of obstruction and gets charged with an error. Crawford was allowed to score the winning run and the game was over.

10. The umpiring crew can and they did, changing the call from a homer to a double. Interestingly, later in that game Morneau drove a ball deep down the line in right that was ruled a home run by umpire Matt Hollowell. However, after another White Sox gripe, the umps huddled to be sure the correct call had been made, and once again they changed their decision. Not at all surprisingly, indignant Minnesota manager Ron Gardenhire, feeling ripped off, argued vehemently and was eventually ejected from the game.

11. The Mets still won since the runner from third base did touch home and Ventura did reach first base safely. Ventura robbed himself of a home run, though, and the final score was decreed to be 4–3 on Ventura's 300-plus foot single; one writer called it a "grand slam-single."

Steve Hirdt, a spokesman for the Elias Sports Bureau, explained to the AP, "The game ends in sudden death when the winning run scores. The only exception is on a home run, assuming the player rounds all the bases. He never rounded the bases." Ventura noted, "I saw it go over and then I just ran to first. As long as I touched first, we won. So that's fine with me."

12. No. First of all, an appeal or, for that matter, a request to play a game under protest would have had to have been made before the team left the field. Secondly, as Chambliss remembered, "A few of them [umpires] told me years later that the run counted because it was the fans that were in the way." In other words, it wasn't Chambliss' fault that he couldn't reach home plate under such unusual circumstances.

13. During that game, part of an interleague "Subway Series" in July 1999, Holbrook ruled himself guilty of interference and Cedeno had to return to second.

★

14. Of course the hitter may bat from either side of the plate. Yes, this happens occasionally when a switch-hitter has had a history of frustration and failure against a given pitcher. For instance, in the third game in the 1999 Division Series between the Atlanta Braves and the Houston Astros, Carl Everett, a switch-hitting outfielder who had great numbers in the regular season (.325, 25 hr, 108 runs driven in) went up against Atlanta lefty Tom Glavine, a Cy Young Award winner. Everett had been stymied to the tune of 1 for 12 lifetime against the tough pitcher so he figured, "What the heck, I'll try batting left-handed against him."

In the first inning, he drew a walk. In his next at bat, he reached on an infield hit, beating the throw to first by about one stride, after he had slapped the ball to second baseman Bret Boone, who had to backhand the ball. Assuming that Everett would have hit the ball in the same location and assuming Boone would have been playing him the same way defensively had Everett been hitting the ball right-handed, Everett would not have beat the ball out. When a player bats left-handed, he is at least a step closer to first base since he begins in the batter's box nearer to first and that can make a difference on many a close play.

For the record, in his third at-bat Everett fanned against Glavine and in the bottom of the 10th inning he came to the plate against another lefty, John Rocker, with the bases loaded. It was a situation in which even a fly ball hit deeply enough for a sacrifice fly would have won the game. This time, relieved that he was not facing his nemesis Glavine, Everett turned around, batted righty, but made a harmless out.

All of this illustrates a point—hitters will make changes, even rather drastic ones if they believe such actions may improve their chances at success.

15. Under normal conditions, such as with the infield not playing in, the ball is ruled dead, the runner is out, but the batter is credited with a hit and is awarded first base. Houston Astros star Craig Biggio once joked, "That's a great team rule because if a guy's struggling and you're [as the runner] going to be out anyway, you might as well kick the ball for the guy so he can get a hit." He laughed and said that while that could happen, it's almost always unintentional.

16. Actually, if the umpire feels Biggio interfered with the play regardless of where he is, he would definitely be ruled out. Biggio has no problem with the interference aspect of the rule, but he felt the placement of the path to be a foolish baseball decision. "Why is that [restraining path] line running down the side of the first base line in foul territory when the base is in fair? So you gotta run [in foul territory] and step in fair; that's pretty stupid."

17. He can not only end the game, he can forfeit it as well. In this case, matters didn't get that extreme and no ump wants to forfeit any contest, let alone a playoff contest. The Yankees had led by a single run entering the ninth, then went on a binge which upset the Fenway spectators, and cruised to a 9–2 victory. Things got so tense and dicey in this rivalry, Yankees wives had to be escorted from the park by police.

18. The first-base ump thought Rolen had snared Biggio's line drive in the air. Basing his ruling on that, he made the correct call. However, when the umps huddled and discussed the play, they sorted things out: It is a double play and Taveras, not forced to leave his base once Biggio was retired, is safe.

19. Yes. The umpires have a whole lot of clout and Weaver's ejection stood. On June 6, 1986, San Diego Padres skipper Steve Boros also was thumbed before the game began. When he met with the umpires pre-game, he tried to hand umpire Charlie Williams a videotape of a play Boros thought Williams had blown the night before. Williams quickly let it be known he would not tolerate such antics.

20. Yes, a man can get kicked out of a game that's over. Ford explained, "You write it up [in an official report] as an ejection, then the league president can do what he wants to do about it."

21. The ump said he would not tolerate "direct profanity [aimed at him]," nor would he allow anyone to "get personal, or delay the game."

22. The mistake must be corrected immediately. The inning is over and Nevin's at-bat is wiped out.

23. In real life the crew chief, Joe West, politely listened to Guillen's plea, but insisted he must bring Politte in. "I screwed up," Guillen admitted. "I told the umpire, 'OK, bring in whoever you want.' It turned out that umpire helped us win the game." Actually, it was the fine pitching of Politte that did the trick. Although left-handed hitters carried a proud .357 batting average to the plate against him, on that day he put out the fire, eventually ending the threat by inducing a double play.

Guillen later joked, "The next time I go out there, I'm going to raise both arms and see who the umpires bring out."

24. The correct rule book call is to award an automatic triple to Terrero, meaning Sanchez's throw and Terrero's dash to the bag had been moot. Some observers assumed Sanchez was not aware of this rare rule, but he confessed he did know of it but made the misplay because he simply got caught up in the action. Sadly for Dodger fans, they had been winning prior to this rare triple but went on to drop the decision to the D-backs. In fact, later in the same inning Sanchez got hurt when he served up a homer to opposing pitcher Javier Vasquez, his first big league homer ever.

25. Thames is out, of course, on the infield fly rule. Monroe and Pena were permitted to advance at their own risk (or, of course, they could have safely stayed at second and first, respectively). When the defense retrieved the ball, but failed to tag either runner, the base runners were ruled safe and remained on second and third since there was no force play once Thames was automatically ruled out.

After the game, Tigers manager Alan Trammell confessed, "We were very fortunate, I'm not going to lie to you. It could have been a triple play, but it worked out in our favor."

26. The play was ruled a home run. ESPN analyst John Kruk, a former outfielder (and first baseman), felt the ruling should have been a four-base error. The Fenway Park official scorer disagreed, feeling it wasn't "a routine play" for the outfielder. Nixon's frustration after the ball nestled into the bullpen seems to have indicated he believed it was a play he needed to and/or could have made.

3

ON TO THE FRONT OFFICE

Having played the role of the manager earlier, it's time now to move up to the front office, don a three-piece suit, and become a team's general manager. Just as kids used to swap baseball cards, it's your turn to wheel and deal and make vital decisions. And remember that nowadays trades aren't the only moves you'd have to make. The age of free agency has complicated the G.M. role a great deal. So, think hard and earn your pay as a front office executive.

1. PITCHER WITH HEAT VS. HOT CORNER ALL-STAR

The New York Mets had trouble finding a quality third baseman basically from their first day of existence. After the 1971 season, they decided to make a trade to fill that need. They acquired veteran Jim Fregosi, a six-time All-Star, from the California Angels in return for Leroy Stanton, Don Rose, Francisco Estrada, and a young flame-throwing pitcher. This wound up being one of the most lopsided trades ever, as the pitcher in question went on to become a Hall of Famer. Imagine what he could have accomplished had he stayed there and worked alongside Tom Seaver and Jerry Koosman. Name the pitcher.

The answer is on page 42.

2. SPEED VS. VETERAN HURLERS

In what is generally regarded as one of the worst front office moves ever, the Chicago Cubs traded for two veteran St. Louis pitchers, Ernie Broglio, and Bobby Shantz, but in return surrendered a future Hall of Fame speed demon. Who was the youngster they gave up on way too early?

The answer is on page 42.

3. PLUGGING A HOLE

In 2004, the Houston Astros had the opportunity to obtain Carlos Beltran from the Kansas City Royals. Now, if you were the Astros general manager, knowing that Beltran was going to be a free agent at the end of the season, would you "rent a player" to help you down the stretch run, perhaps propelling you into the postseason?

The answer is on page 42.

4. SWAP HIM?

Just days before the 1982 season began, the Texas Rangers sent a hard-hitting outfielder to the Montreal Expos for Larry Parrish and Dave Hostetler. Parrish gave the Rangers six productive seasons, including two with 100 or more RBI. Hostetler spent three years with Texas, with '82 being his best showing (only .232, but with 67 RBI). Even though the Expos new outfielder lasted only two seasons with them, in 1982 he led the National League in hits, doubles, runs driven in, and batting average. Whether this deal favored the Expos or the Rangers is debatable; your call is to identify the man who went on to win the batting crown in his debut season with the Expos. Was it: A) Al Oliver; B) Andre Dawson; C) Tim Raines; or D) Warren Cromartie?

The answer is on page 43.

5. UNIQUE TRADE

Only once in the annals of the game has a reigning batting crown winner been traded for the winner of the home run crown. Name the principals in this deal.

The answer is on page 43.

6. A-ROD WORTH IT?

On January 26, 2001, the Texas Rangers signed Alex Rodriquez as a free agent, almost exactly three months after he was granted free agency status, cutting his ties with the Mariners. He stayed deep in the heart of the Lone Star state until February 16, 2004, when he was peddled to the Yankees in exchange for Alfonso Soriano and cash. During his three-season Texas stay, he earned a staggering $66 million. Was he worth all that loot?

The answer is on page 44.

7. ANOTHER MORTGAGING THE FUTURE SCENARIO

Down the stretch run of the 1987 pennant race, the Detriot Tigers felt that if they could pick up a dependable veteran pitcher, they could win their division. After trade talks between Atlanta and Detroit went on for some time, a deal was consummated. The Tigers got veteran Doyle Alexander for a young John Smoltz. Would you have made this swap?

The answer is on page 44.

8. TURNABOUT

The 2003 Detroit Tigers were positively hapless, but they were able to transform themselves into a respectable team in just one year by making a few moves. They picked up a bullpen closer in Ugueth Urbina, but their acquisitions of an established star behind the plate and a fine shortstop were key pickups. Name either of these men.

The answer is on page 45.

9. BACK-TO-BACK MVP AWARDS

In 1972, the Cincinnatti Reds were ripped by their fans for shipping Lee May, Tommy Helms, and Jimmy Stewart to Houston. The Reds added four players to their roster who would go on to form a nucleus for their success in the "Big Red Machine" era, proving once more that trades cannot be evaluated on the spot. In addition to Ed Armrister, Jack Billingham, and Cesar Geronimo, what future Hall of Fame infielder and winner of consecutive MVP trophies did the Reds gain in this huge trade?

The answer is on page 45.

10. ANOTHER BIG FAUX PAS

The Philadelphia Phillies gave up on this young right-hander when they made a deal with the Cubs in 1966. Chicago shrewdly surrendered aging pitchers Bob Buhl and Larry Jackson, and both were finished within three years. In the mean time, their new acquisition won 147 games as a Cub, won the 1971 Cy Young Award, and mowed down 1, 808 batters while with the Cubbies. Name this pitcher.

The answer is on page 45.

★ CHAPTER 3 ANSWERS ★

1. It was a young Nolan Ryan. Over his time spent with the Mets, he won just 29 games; over his next three seasons with the Angels, he averaged just over 20 victories a year with untouchable strikeout totals: 329, the all-time record high of 383, and 367. He was off and running, on his way to 324 wins and a staggering 5,714 whiffs. In the meantime, Fregosi lasted only one full season (.232 and just 32 RBI) with the Mets before they dumped him in 1973 after only 45 games.

2. The Cubs served Lou Brock up on a platter to the Cardinals, where he stayed as an institution from the day of the trade in 1964 through the end of his career in 1979. Over that span he registered over 3,000 hits, burgled 938 bases—the all-time best until Rickey Henderson came along—and helped guide the Cards to three World Series appearances. Broglio and Shantz were pretty good pitchers, but by the time of the transaction they were over the hill. Broglio won seven games for the Cubs in two and a half seasons and Shantz lasted only 20 games (0–1) for Chicago.

3. When a team makes a move that may help them short term, but perhaps hurts them long range, they are said to have "mortgaged their future." In some cases, when trying to determine if a move was worth it or not, one should wait many years before looking back to make a judgment.

In the Astros' case, you decide, but here are the facts to date: 1) They made the playoffs with Beltran contributing big time. Overall, he drove in 104 runs and fell just short of becoming the fourth member of the 40 home run/40 stolen base club. In the Astros uniform, he hit 23 homers and scored 70 runs in a mere 90 games. 2) For the first time since their inception in 1962, the Astros made it to the second round of the postseason and did so largely thanks to Beltran's record four homers in the Division Series versus Atlanta. 3) Ultimately, Houston lost to St. Louis, but only after Beltran tied playoff records with his totals of eight homers and 14 RBI to go with his .435 average. 4) Before the start of 2005, the Astros lost Beltran through free agency to the New York Mets, who agreed to pay him over $11.5 million for the 2005 season.

4. A. Al Oliver. Incidentally, twice in baseball history a team has swapped a player during a season and that man went on to win that season's batting title. It happened in 1932 when the Tigers sent Dale Alexander (after he had only 16 at bats with them) to the Red Sox and in 1947 when Harry "The Hat" Walker was dealt from the Cardinals (after just 25 at bats there) to the Phillies.

5. Prior to the 1960 season, Rocky Colavito was sent packing by general manager Frank "Trader" Lane to Detroit for Harvey Kuenn. Kuenn was coming off a marvelous .353 season, but Cleveland fans didn't care about that—they were livid. The beloved Colavito had just drilled 42 homers and chased home 111 runs. Colavito, too, was outraged. He commented, "The trade came as a great shock. It was a trade that never should have happened. I got dumped."

What made matters worse was Colavito went on to average more that 32 homers a year for the next seven seasons. By contrast, Kuenn lasted only one year with the Indians.

6. It's your call, but, once more, here are some basic facts: Over that span the Rangers were in fourth place each year, failing each season to break .500. Over the eight previous seasons before his arrival they finished first four times, second once, third two times, and fourth once, in 2000. The year he departed the Rangers went from fourth to third place in the standings. Clearly, he was no savior.

He was, however, as always, a superstar. His stats glistened: He played 162 games each year despite laboring under the draining, blistering, and unforgiving Texas sun. He crushed 52, 57, and 47 home runs and delivered well over 100 RBI yearly with a high of 142 in 2002. He hit over .300 with a slugging percentage over .600 during his tenure as a Ranger. What more could he have done? Was it his fault the club didn't have enough support to win more frequently? Again, in this case, it's your call.

7. One can look at this deal two ways: Any chance you have to make it to the playoffs with a legitimate chance to win it all, you must seize the day. From the day of the deal, August 12, through the end of the season, Alexander, who had been 5–10 for the Braves, sizzled. His unblemished 9–0 slate with a spectacular ERA of 1.53 helped ignite the Tigers who won the East Division, but they fell short of a World Series apearance when the Twins knocked them off in the ALCS.

The trade has to be considered a flop if one reviews what Smoltz went on to achieve. Eighteen years after the swap, Smoltz had 172 wins and 154 saves for Atlanta. Both of those figures are more than any Tigers pitcher could muster over that time frame. As a matter of fact, the most victories the most successful Tigers hurler accumulated over that span was 61 by Frank Tanana, some 111 fewer than Smoltz! He is the only man ever to be effective enough as a starter to notch 15 shutouts while also being so sharp as a reliever he compiled 150-plus saves. Not only that, the 1996 Cy Young Award winner has been a mainstay of the Braves who, through 2005, made it to the playoffs every year since 1991. He is, in fact, the only player to have been a part of each and every one of those title teams. Finally, from May 29, 2002 until May 26, 2003, the Braves never lost a game in which Smoltz pitched. That covered a period of 72 straight wins, a big league record. In short, Alexander was a big help for one year, but Smoltz has been "money" for an eon.

8. The Tigers front office aggressively went after and signed catcher Ivan Rodriguez as a free agent to a hefty cotract (just over $6.5 million in 2004) and picked up new short-stop Carlos Guillen.

Shortly after the All-Star break, on July 18, 2004, the Tigers had surpassed their victory total from the entire 2003 season and still had two and a half months left to play. Sure, they were only playing near the .500 level, but it was a considerable improvement over their showing in 2003 when they set a new American League record for losses, going 43–119. They also established a record for the fewest games needed to go beyond their win total from the previous year, needing just 91 games, some 15 fewer than the previous record-holders. In all, their win total ascended by nearly 30, up to 72 victories in 2004.

9. The future Hall of Fame infielder and MVP trophy winner was second baseman Joe Morgan.

★

10. The Cub who won the 1971 Cy Young Award was Fergie Jenkins.

est your knowledge of star players by listening to clues and identifying the "speaker."

1. HIT 'EM WHERE THEY ARE

My strike zone is as big as my eyes. That is to say, I like to swing at virtually any pitch, anywhere—I've been known to hoist pitches from down near the top of my spikes for homers and I've been known to tee off on pitches up to my eyes. The results are the same, awesome. I won an MVP Award in the American League and I've hit for power and average every season since my real season in the Bigs, not counting 1996 when I was up for a brief "sip of coffee." In fact, the .302 I hit in 1997 is the lowest I've hit in the majors. As for my power numbers, in my first eight seasons I've hit 34 or more homers six times, the same amount of times I've driven home 100 or more runs. Who am I?

The answer is on page 52.

2. THEY CALL ME "PAPI"

My nickname alone might give my identity away. I am a dead pull hitter who amasses homers the way Disney's Scrooge McDuck piled up moolah. What a treat it was to be a part (a big part, with 41 homers and 139 RBI) of the 2004 world champion Boston Red Sox after finding my first big league success with the Minnesota Twins as a first sacker and a designated hitter. Can you ID me?

The answer is on page 52.

3. I CAN DO IT ALL

I have won Gold Glove awards, but am more famous for my bat. In 2005, I became only the fourth man ever to hit 500 or more homers while also owning 3,000 or more hits. I did so while in the Baltimore Orioles jersey. Who am I?

The answer is on page 52.

4. PERFECTION

In 1965 Chicago Cubs pitcher Bob Hendley *lost* a 1–0 one-hitter. Hendley lost because I, a Los Angeles Dodgers pitcher, threw a perfect game that day. Only Lou Johnson's seventh inning double prevented this game from being a double no-hitter, something that has happened only once in the history of the game. In the fifth inning, Johnson had drawn a walk and scored after a sacrifice, a steal, and a Cubs error. Clue: I already had thrown three other no-hitters before my '65 masterpiece. Who am I?

The answer is on page 52.

5. WHAT A COINCIDENCE!

I am a .303 lifetime hitter, but also have the distinction of making the final out in two no-hitters authored by the same pitcher, doing so in 1963 and 1965. I guided the Milwaukee Brewers to a World Series appearance in 1982, losing in seven to the Cardinals. Who am I? *The answer is on page 52.*

6. HIT ME, I HIT YOU

I pitched alongside Sandy Koufax, once holding out with him in an unprecedented two-man power ploy to get a better contract from the Dodgers. Mike Shannon once spoke about my fearlessness and my willingness to brush back and even bean batters to get my message across that I was in control. He said that I "would consider an intentional walk a waste of three pitches. If he wants to put you on base, he can hit you with one." Who am I?

The answer is on page 52.

7. SUPERLATIVE SOUTHPAW

My "out" pitch was my sharp-as-a-straight-razor slider. I set a record with 19 strikeouts in a 1969 game (since broken), with many of the K's coming on sliders.

I attributed much of my success to grueling workouts, which included stretching, lifting, and martial arts work. Final clue: In 1972, even though my Philadelphia Phillies were a terrible team, I won an astounding 27 games, accounting for almost 50 percent of my team's measly 59 victories. Who am I?   *The answer is on page 53.*

8. HE'S A SLAMMER

I began my big league career with the Texas Rangers, whose co-managing general partner was George W. Bush. In an ill-fated trade, I was sent to the White Sox. My most recent team has been the Orioles. This next clue should give my identity away: From 1998 through 2001 I averaged almost exactly 61 homers per season with blistering totals of 66, 63, 50, and 64 round-trippers. Who am I?

The answer is on page 53.

9. GIVE 'EM THE THUMB, TWICE!

Odd one: In 1946, having retired as a member of the 500 home run club, I became the first manager to be ejected from both ends of a doubleheader. That day my New York Giants were swept by the Pittsburgh Pirates. Who am I?

The answer is on page 53.

10. 3,000 HITS AND COUNTING

On June 9, 1914, I became the first man ever to reach the 3,000 hits plateau and I went on to stroke an additional 430 before I hung up my cleats. Who am I?

The answer is on page 53.

11. HOME RUNS GALORE

Many of my myriad home runs did not fly majestically out of parks, but rather followed a line drive trajectory as they cleared the walls. They still tell the story of the time I lifted a line drive over the shortstop who leaped to try to snag the ball; seconds later, the ball, still rising, left the park. My bat was said to be quicker than a University of Miami defensive back. I hold countless records, including the most runs driven in over a career, 2,297, which works out to an average of 99.9 RBI for each of my 23 seasons in the majors. Who am I?   *The answer is on page 53.*

12. ANOTHER HOME RUN KING

When I came to the plate, third basemen tended to position themselves very deep, almost as if they were a softball rover in the outfield. No wonder, I pulled the ball as hard as a Dick Butkus forearm smash. One longtime fan observed, "All you have to do to know who the wicked pull hitters are is look at where the third base coach stands when a guy's up and there's no traffic to direct." When I hit, my third base coach always distanced himself from me and the really hot corner; at times, it seemed like he wished he was a bullpen coach, rather than a base coach.

My biggest accomplishment came when I was with the Cardinals, but I had been a Rookie of the Year with the Oakland A's in 1987, setting home run records early on. I wound up with 583 lifetime homers. Who am I?

The answer is on page 53.

13. PHILLY SLUGGER

Lee Smith made this observation about me: "He had some of the quickest and strongest hands as I've ever seen on a hitter. He was unbelievable. You could make good pitches and he'd just golf balls right off the ground." I was with the Phillies for my entire 18-year career. I retired in 1989 as an eight-time home run king and with nearly 1,600 runs driven in. Who am I?   *The answer is on page 54.*

14. GLOWING WORDS

My one-time Angels teammate Doug DeCinces commented, "The difference between this guy and the rest of us is that when we get hot, we go up to .300. When he gets hot, he goes up to .500." Former infielder Alan Bannister was cited in *Baseball Quotations* as joking, "He's the only guy I know who can go four-for-three." Finally, pitcher Ken Holtzman observed, "He has an uncanny ability to move the ball around as if the bat were some kind of magic wand." I was always aware of where the defense played me and did what it took to get on base—be it lay down a bunt or lash out a line drive. I wound up with 3,053 lifetime hits. Who am I?

The answer is on page 54.

15. CAN'T WHIFF HIM

A Hall of Fame outfielder, I was extremely difficult to strike out. Over my illustrious career, spent entirely as a New York Yankee, I struck out just 369 times. I also hit .325 lifetime with 361 home runs. Usually batters with some clout will fan frequently—it's an occupational hazard. In my case, though, things were quite different. My ratio of almost exactly one home run for every strikeout is the lowest in the history of the game for men with 300 or more homers. Who am I? *The answer is on page 54.*

16. CAN'T WHIFF HIM, PART II

I am second, trailing only a teammate of mine, for the best career ratio of homers-to-strikeouts as I hit 358 homers and went down on strikes only 415 times. My lifetime average was .285 and my other achievements, including those as a manager, did earn a spot for me in the Hall of Fame as well. I had a reputation for hacking away at pitches almost regardless of their locations, but I got the job done. I even took home three MVP Awards and was named to 15 All-Star contests. Who am I?

The answer is on page 54.

17. TAG TEAM

Two men from the same team seldom wind up one-two for the RBI leadership in a league, and it's even more rare for teammates to tie for the lead. In 1928, for instance, Lou Gehrig and Babe Ruth shared the lead with 142 runs driven in each. The next time that feat occurred was in 1949 when two Red Sox players drove in a whopping 159 runs apiece. I did this and my teammate who matched me was Vern Stephens.

Additionally, I am one of only two men to win the Triple Crown on two occasions. Ironically, I didn't win the MVP in either of my Triple Crown seasons, but I did win that trophy twice. Who am I? *The answer is on page 54.*

18. FORMER KING OF K

For a baseball eon, my lifetime strikeout record stood insurmountable. Finally, it was toppled when Nolan Ryan fanned his 3,509th victim. They say my fastball is still among the swiftest of all time and that, coupled with my sidearm delivery, helped me amass 110 shutouts, still the most ever. I spent 21 seasons with the Washington Senators and the last time I took the field, way back on September 30, 1927, was as a pinch-hitter (only six pitchers ever hit more than my 24 lifetime homers) in the same contest that Babe Ruth tagged his 60th home run. Final clue: I was one of the five charter members inducted into the Hall of Fame. Who am I? *The answer is on page 54.*

1. Vladimir Guerrero.

2. David Ortiz.

3. Rafael Palmeiro, joining Hank Aaron, Willie Mays, and Eddie Murphy.

4. Sandy Koufax, a man who had engineered no-hitters in 1962, 1963, and 1964, then topped it off with his perfecto. In that game, Koufax struck out 14, including six of the final seven Cubs hitters, lifting his record to 22–7. His four no-hitters stood as the all-time record until it was snapped by Nolan Ryan, who has seven. Hendley ended the year at 4–4 and was a sub-.500 pitcher lifetime (48–52).

5. Harvey Kuenn. Amazingly, both times Kuenn made the final out was in no-hitters featuring Sandy Koufax on the mound—in the second instance, the no-no was, in fact, a perfect game.

★

6. "Double D," Don Drysdale, like Koufax, a Hall of Famer. Drysdale set a record in 1968 when he blanked opponents for 58 straight innings. In 1965, he led the Dodgers' entire team in batting when he was the only .300 hitter in their lineup. That same year, he tied his own National League record for the most homers hit in a season by a pitcher (seven).

7. 300-game winner Steve Carlton, owner of six 20-win seasons. He was also the first man to accumulate four Cy Young Awards and remains the second winningest southpaw ever, trailing only Warren Spahn.

8. "Slammin" Sammy Sosa.

9. Mel Ott, yet another Hall of Famer. Ott was his league's top home run hitter six times after breaking into the major leagues as a 17-year-old.

10. Honus Wagner of the Pittsburgh Pirates. As a trivia note, Wagner became the first player to have his signature branded into a Louisville Slugger bat back in 1905. Wagner is also noted for having hit over .300 for 17 straight seasons, beginning in 1897 when he was a mere rookie.

11. Hank Aaron, most famous, of course, for shattering Ruth's lifetime home run record of 714—Aaron ended his magnificent career with 755 shots. A lesser known record is the one he holds with Eddie Mathews, which broke a standard formerly held by Babe Ruth and Lou Gehrig for the most homers hit by two teammates.

12. Mark McGwire, who broke the former single season home-run record of 61 when he crushed 70 homers in 1998 (only to see Barry Bonds breeze by that total in 2001 with 73 blows).

13. Mike Schmidt, one of a few men to win back-to-back MVP Awards. Schmidt entered the Hall of Fame when he received 444 votes out of 460 ballots cast in 1995. The Hall of Fame website boasts of Schmidt possessing, "An unprecedented combination of power and defense . . ." By the time his career ended, he had punished the ball 548 times for home runs, and his 48 homers in 1980 remain the most ever in a season by a third sacker.

14. Rod Carew. Only Ty Cobb (with 12, the all-time high), Tony Gwynn, and Honus Wagner own more batting titles than his seven. He also reached the .300 level 15 years in a row.

15. Joe DiMaggio. Also known as the "Yankee Clipper," DiMaggio was a three-time MVP winner but probably remains most famous for his astonishing record 56-game hitting streak accomplished in 1941.

16. Yogi Berra, also a three-time AL MVP winner.

17. Ted Williams. Clearly he was a tremendous hitter for both power (521 lifetime blows) and average (.344 career; only seven men—most of them from the early days of the game—hit higher than Williams, including Ty Cobb's best ever .367).

18. Walter Johnson. His 417 career victories still stands second on the all-time list, trailing only Cy Young's 511 wins. Truly one of the best hitting pitchers ever, his astronomical .433 batting average in 1925, racked up very late in his career and, at the age of 37, set a still-untouched record for pitchers. For that matter, no everyday player has hit that high, either.

5
FIRSTS AND LASTS

See how vivid your memory is when it comes to trivia about beginnings and endings, be it of seasons, players' careers, and more.

1. WHAT A START!

Who is the only man to fire a no-hitter on Opening Day? He was a Cleveland Indians great and his performance took place in 1940 versus the White Sox. Name this man.

The answer is on page 64.

2. CHRISTENING YANKEE STADIUM

The first game ever played at Yankee Stadium took place on April 18, 1923. Who hit the first homer ever at that venue? *The answer is on page 64.*

3. LET THERE BE LIGHTS

Guess the date of the first Opening Day played under lights: A) 1930; B) 1940; C) 1950; or D) 1960.

The answer is on page 64.

4. LET THERE BE A DH

The first use of a designated hitter took place on Opening Day when a Yankee stepped into the box and drew a walk. Name that man or, within three years, guess when this occurred. *The answer is on page 64.*

5. HISTORY IS MADE

The Atlanta versus Cincinnati lid-lifter of April 4, 1974, featured an historic event. Jack Billingham delivered a pitch that a member of the Braves pulled crisply for a monumental record-tying homer. Who was the batter and what was the significance of the home run?

The answer is on page 64.

6. GIVE ME THE BALL

In 1985, this pitcher made his record-setting 15th Opening Day start. Name this three-time Cy Young Award winner, who was also the Rookie of the Year in 1967 with the Mets.

The answer is on page 64.

7. A FIRST "FIRST"

Nicknamed "Dewey," this man also made history, doing so on April 7, 1986, when he smacked the very first pitch of the new season for a round tripper, connecting for the Red Sox against Jack Morris and the Tigers. Clue: his initials are D.E.

The answer is on page 64.

8. PRESIDENTIAL FIRST

Tough one: Within 10 years, guess the first time a United States President threw out the first ball on Opening Day. If you prefer, guess which President it was.

The answer is on page 65.

9. ANOTHER TRADITION

For decade after decade, this team had the honor of hosting the very first game of each season. They were given that privilege since that city was home to baseball's first professional baseball team. Name this city.

The answer is on page 65.

10. HE LOVES OPENERS

What man hit more home runs on Opening Day than any other man? Clue: His most famous homer in an Opener came when he was a player-manager for the Indians in 1975. *The answer is on page 65.*

11. A FAMOUS "FIRSTS"

What team was the first one to sport an all switch-hitting infield? Clue: The four-man crew was in the lineup most days during the 1965 and 1966 seasons for a National League team. *The answer is on page 65.*

12. ANOTHER "FIRST"

What player became the first man ever to be selected for one All-Star team yet wound up playing for the other squad? Clue: This happened in the 21st century, and the player involved was an outfielder. *The answer is on page 65.*

13. A FINAL "FIRST"

Who was the first player ever to hit 30 or more homers in a season; the first to reach 40+ homers; and the first to attain the 50 home-run plateau? *The answer is on page 65.*

14. ALL-STAR FIRST

What was the first brother combination to play in an All-Star contest? *The answer is on page 66.*

15. BROTHERS

Speaking of brothers, on September 15, 1963, the San Francisco Giants lineup included a defensive alignment of three brothers covering the outfield, a "first" that's never been duplicated. Can you name the brothers? Clue: One of them produced a son who has done quite well in the majors. Further, that father has also been his son's manager at the big league level. They were even on the NL All-Star team in 2005; the father as a coach, the son as, what else, an outfielder. *The answer is on page 66.*

16. FATHER'S DAY MASTERPIECE

On Father's Day of 1964 (June 21), a Philadelphia Phillies pitcher threw a no-hitter to become the first man to record a no-hitter in both leagues. Who was this righty?

The answer is on page 66.

17. OLD MAN ON THE HILL

How old was Satchel Paige when he recorded his first big league complete game: A) 40; B) 42; C) 44; or D) 46?

The answer is on page 66.

18. N.L. BREAKS THE FUTILITY STREAK

The first All-Star game was held in 1933. When was the first time a National League team won the event in an American League ballpark: A) 1934; B) 1945; C) 1948; or D) 1950?

The answer is on page 66.

19. PENNANT "FIRST"

Who was the first big league manager to win a pennant in both leagues?

The answer is on page 67.

20. CAREER BEGINNINGS

Moving to starts of careers, rather than seasons, see if you can match the sluggers with the team these sluggers broke in with:

A. Babe Ruth
B. Hank Aaron
C. Barry Bonds
D. Willie Mays
E. Frank Robinson

A. Milwaukee Braves
B. Pittsburgh Pirates
C. Boston Red Sox
D. Cincinnati Reds
E. New York Giants

The answers are on page 67.

21. MORE CAREER BEGINNINGS

Next, try to match these .300-caliber hitters to the teams with which they began their major league careers:

A. Larry Walker
B. Sean Casey
C. Rod Carew
D. Rafael Palmeiro
E. Alex Rodriguez

A. Seattle Mariners
B. Chicago Cubs
C. Cleveland Indians
D. Montreal Expos
E. Minnesota Twins

The answers are on page 67.

22. FINAL DAY DRAMATICS

The 1950 regular season had a dramatic conclusion in the National League. The Phillies and Dodgers had raged through a hard-fought pennant race which came down to the last game of the year, which just happened to be between these two pennant-hungry clubs. Even then, at the end of nine innings they were deadlocked at one run apiece. Finally, in the tenth inning, a Philadelphia outfielder took Don Newcombe deep to win it all as the Phillies earned their first trip to the World Series since 1915. Tough one: Who hit the game-winning homer? His initials are D.S. and his father, George, was a Hall of Famer who had twice hit .400, topping out at a sparkling .420 in 1922.

The answer is on page 67.

23. ODDITY

As the 1954 season wound down, Casey Stengel found himself in an unusual plight. His Yankees, normally the American League champs, had been eliminated from the pennant chase. Facing the Athletics, who were about to play their final game ever in Philadelphia, before the team was uprooted and moved to Kansas City, Stengel shook up his lineup. Bill "Moose" Skowron played second base instead of his normal first base position and center fielder Mickey Mantle handled shortstop duties, something he did seven times over his 18 years in the majors. Finally, Stengel's usual starting catcher played third for the only time in his 19-year career. Name that famous catcher.

The answer is on page 67.

24. PERFECT ENDING

Back on September 30, 1984, an Angels pitcher tossed baseball's only perfect game on the final day of a season. The 6' 7" righty dazzled the Rangers that day, 1–0, using a scant 94 pitches and going to a three-ball count just once. His initials are M.W. Name this "perfectionist."

The answer is on page 67.

25. PERFECT ENDING, PART II

In 1975, the manager of the Oakland A's decided to use several pitchers to wrap up the season simply because he wanted to give each of those men some work prior to the ALCS. The result was quite favorable—his four-man "staff" tossed a no-hitter. This manager's initials are A.D. Can you identify him?

The answer is on page 68.

26. NOTCHING #300

This Hall of Fame pitcher reached his 300th win on the season finale in 1985. Facing the Blue Jays, this 46-year-old Yankees righty (who broke in with the Milwaukee Braves in 1964) worked a four-hit shutout. Clue: He didn't use his specialty pitch until the ninth inning, trying to prove he could win without his unusual pitch.

The answer is on page 68.

27. FAMOUS FINISH

One of the most memorable events from a final game came in 1941 when Ted Williams, perched comfortably on a .400-plus average, refused to sit out a season-ending doubleheader. He not only played both ends, he banged out six hits to elevate his batting average to a heady .406 mark. Who was his manager who offered to let Williams rest on the pines? Clues: He is a Hall of Famer, a great Red Sox hitter himself, with the initials J.C.

The answer is on page 68.

28. STRANGE BATTING CROWN BATTLE

As the 1910 season wound down, Nap Lajoie and his Cleveland Naps (nicknamed in honor of Lajoie) played St. Louis in a doubleheader on October 9. The popular Lajoie trailed a despised player for the league lead in batting by a wide spread. Lajoie needed an eight-for-nine showing to snare the batting title. Thanks to some help from a cooperative Browns defense, that is exactly what he got.

St. Louis manager Jack O'Connor instructed his rookie third baseman to play deep, way out by the outfield grass, a defensive deployment that came into play by Lajoie's third at bat. His first two times to the plate produced a clean triple and a bunt single on a ball fielded by shortstop Bobby Wallace. Things changed, though, over his next seven trips to the plate as Lajoie placed bunts down the third base line—six resulted in hits.

Lajoie had, it appeared, won the batting crown. However, the American League, embarrassed by St. Louis' shenanigans, eventually took action. On October 15, league president Ban Johnson announced that, after final calculations had been made, Lajoie had actually lost the title by a microscopic gap of .384944 to the other star's .384084. What player was awarded the batting crown?

The answer is on page 69.

29. BIZARRE ENDING

What was the only year in which there was no true resolution to the season? On August 11 of this year the season play simply screeched to a frustrating halt due to a labor dispute. By September 14 the word came: The season and the World Series had been wiped out. Was it A) 1970; B) 1977; C) 1994); or D) 1998?

The answer is on page 69.

30. FOREIGN SOIL

On March 29, 2000, the earliest Opening Day ever took place. The Mets dropped a 5–3 decision to the Cubs in the first big league game played outside of North America. Trivia items abounded: The first "overseas" batter was Eric Young; the first such homer was swatted by Shane Andrews; and the win went to Jon Lieber. Your question: Where was this game held: A) Italy; B) Brazil; C) China; or D) Japan?   *The answer is on page 69.*

31. END OF CAREERS QUIZ

Moving from season finales to career closings, here's a quiz concerning what team star players ended their careers with. Some teams match up with more than one player.

A. Hank Aaron	A. Cleveland Indians
B. Eddie Mathews	B. Detroit Tigers
C. Warren Spahn	C. Oakland A's
D. Dick Allen	D. Kansas City Royals
E. Willie Mays	E. Boston Braves
F. Babe Ruth	F. New York Mets
G. Frank Robinson	G. Milwaukee Brewers
H. Billy Williams	
I. Dave Winfield	
J. Harmon Killebrew	*The answers are on page 70.*

32. A FIRST AND A LAST

Who was the first ambidextrous pitcher in pro ball? The last one?   *The answers are on page 70.*

1. Bob Feller. His feat resulted in a peculiar bit of trivia—the no-hitter marked the first time ever that every hitter finished a game with exactly the same batting average he had coming into that contest, .000!

2. Babe Ruth hit the first-ever Yankee Stadium round-tripper, helping the Yanks knock off the Red Sox. Ruth also homered in his final Opener in 1935 when he made his NL debut with the Boston Braves.

3. B. On April 17, 1950, the St. Louis Cardinals hosted the Pirates and captured a 4–2 decision in the first night time Opener.

4. The first DH ever was Ron Bloomberg of the New York Yankees and the date was April 6, 1973.

5. Hank Aaron hit his 714th homer off Billingham to tie Babe Ruth's lifetime total.

6. Tom Seaver had the 15 Opening Day starts.

7. Dwight Evans was the first man to blast the season's first offering for a home run.

8. The first President to launch Opening Day by throwing out a ceremonial pitch was William Howard Taft on April 14, 1910.

9. Cincinnati traditionally hosted each season's lid-lifter. Their streak ran from 1890–1965.

10. Frank Robinson, with eight home runs, ranks first for lifetime Opening Day circuit shots.

11. The Los Angeles Dodgers fielded four switch-hitters around their infield: Wes Parker was at first base, the second sacker was Jim Lefebvre, Maury Wills handled the shortstop duties, and Jim Gilliam played the hot corner.

12. Carlos Beltran was voted to the American League squad in 2004 for his fine showing with the Kansas City Royals before he was swapped to the Houston Astros. When Ken Griffey, Jr. was injured just prior to the mid-summer classic, Beltran was selected to fill the void and man center field for the National League.

13. The first man to reach the 30, 40, 50, and throw in the 60 home run level, was the king of clout, Babe Ruth.

14. On July 8, 1941, Joe and Dom DiMaggio both appeared in that year's All-Star game. That game, incidentally, also marked the first time a player hit two homers—Arky Vaughn of the Pittsburgh Pirates hit two out that day.

15. The brothers were the Alous: Jesus, Matty, and Felipe, whose son is Moises.

16. Jim Bunning threw a no-hitter in the AL for Detroit and the 1964 classic with the Phillies. By the way, his catcher on that Father's Day, Gus Triandos, became the first man to have caught a no-hitter in both circuits.

17. B. Paige, major league baseball's oldest rookie ever, was believed to be 42 years old (details of his exact age are sketchy) when he chalked up his first complete game on August 13, 1948.

18. D. The first National League All-Star win in the enemy's park didn't come until 1950. Even then it took 14 draining innings and a Red Schoendienst homer in that frame to eke out a 4–3 victory.

19. Joe McCarthy was the first skipper to nail down pennants in both leagues.

20. Babe Ruth began with C) the Boston Red Sox. Aaron started with A) the Milwaukee Braves. Bonds was originally a member of B) the Pittsburgh Pirates. Mays' trek through the majors began in the uniform of E) the New York Giants. And Robinson started out with D) the Cincinnati Reds.

21. Larry Walker began with D) the Montreal Expos. Casey started as a member of C) the Cleveland Indians. The Minnesota Twins (E) gave Carew his first shot in the bigs. Palmeiro was originally a Chicago Cub (B). A-Rod's big league origin was with A) the Seattle Mariners.

22. Dick Sisler's homer won the NL flag for St. Louis.

23. Yogi Berra was Stengel's pick to play third that day. Many people forget, but Berra also played in the outfield in 260 contests. In fact, trivia experts recall the historic home run hit by Bill Mazeroski to clinch the 1960 World Series sailed over Berra in left field.

24. Mike Witt threw the season-ending perfect game.

25. The combined "no-no" took place under Alvin Dark's leadership. His starter, Vida Blue, toiled for the first five frames, then departed despite surrendering nary a hit. He was followed by Glenn Abbott, who retired the California Angels one-two-three in the sixth, and Paul Linblad, who turned in a perfect seventh inning. By that point everyone was aware of the potential no-hitter. Closer Rollie Fingers then blazed his way through the final six batters, concluding the classic by retiring pinch hitter Mickey Rivers on a groundout.

Incidentally, at the end of the 1949 season the St. Louis Browns, during the first game of a twinbill, decided to throw nine pitchers against the Chicago White Sox, using one man per inning. The parade of pitchers featured Ned Garver, Joe Ostrowski, Cliff Fannin, Tom Ferrick, Karl Drews, Bill Kennedy, the eventual loser, along with Al Papai, Red Embree, and Dick Starr.

26. It was Phil Niekro, master of the knuckleball. He whipped out that pitch just three times in all, doing so when he whiffed the game's last batter, Jeff Burroughs. Niekro later commented in an autobiography, "I always wanted to pitch a whole game without throwing a knuckleball because people thought I couldn't get anyone out without doing so." As for his decision to unveil the pitch to secure his 300th win, he simply stated, "I figured there was no other way to finish the game than to use the pitch that got me there."

27. Williams' manager the year he hit .406 was Joe Cronin.

28. The reviled player Lajoie had nearly snatched the crown from was Ty Cobb. Not only that, the day after Lajoie banged out his eight hits, seemingly enough to win the title, he received a congratulatory telegram from eight of Cobb's teammates—that's how deeply Cobb was hated!

Decades later the issue still wasn't totally resolved as researchers discovered Cobb had accidentally been given credit for two hits he had not really earned that year. Due to a double entry of statistics from a game in which he had gone 2-for-3, Cobb's listed average was higher than Lajoie's, but truly it wasn't. Still, to this day, although some sources differ as to the exact numbers these men put up, the official record book shows Cobb, with a .385 batting average, to be the batting champ of 1910.

29. C. The shortened season mentioned was in 1994.

30. D. The historic opener took place in Tokyo, Japan, a logical venue in light of the recent influx into the United States of Japanese stars such as Seattle's Ichiro Suzuki and Tokyo native Hideki Matsui of the Yankees.

31. Here are the answers:

Hank Aaron ended his glorious career with G) the Milwaukee Brewers. Eddie Mathews finished with B) the Detroit Tigers. Warren Spahn finished with F) the New York Mets.

Dick Allen's last campaign was with C) the Oakland A's. Willie Mays also ended it all with F) the Mets. Babe Ruth, like home run rivals Aaron and Mays, finished his career in the same city he had begun in, but with a different team: E) the Boston Braves.

Frank Robinson's final team as a player was A) the Cleveland Indians. Billy Williams last suited up with C) the Oakland A's. David Winfield called it quits as A) an Indian. Harmon Killebrew's last port of call was Kansas City (D).

32. The first professional to pitch ambidextrously was Tony Mullane way back on July 18, 1882, while hurling for Louisville. Mullane, normally a righty, faced Baltimore and, when a batch of three straight lefties came to the plate, Mullane, according to a newspaper report of the day, "changed his delivery from right-handed to left, and puzzled the batters considerably."

The most recent pitcher who threw both ways in a big league game was Greg Harris of the Montreal Expos. As the 1995 season wound down, Harris, a natural righty (who was listed as a switch-hitter), became the second post-1900 pitcher to do this feat. He worked a scoreless ninth inning of the September 28 game versus Cincinnati and did so using a specially constructed six-finger glove that allowed him to switch easily from one hand to the other.

Also, in the spring of 1990 a pitcher for St. Leo College in Florida started four games over a six-day span. What enabled him to toil so often was his ambidexterity.

6
UNUSUAL PLAYS AND ODDITIES
OF THE GAME

Take a seventh inning stretch from the quizzes and relax here. Over the years a slew of strange things have transpired on major league baseball diamonds. Here's a handful of such moments.

BOOTING THE BALL

Former big leaguer Rico Brogna dug through a ton of memories to come up with a very bizarre play. "I'm not sure what year it was, I think it might have been Paul O'Neill's last year in Cincinnati [1992]. It's one of the most amazing plays I've ever seen. The game was on the line—I believe it would've been the winning run for whoever the Reds were playing that day and the ball is hit to right field where O'Neill bobbled it, he juggled it, and then, in frustration, just kind of kicked it as if to say, 'The game's probably going to end now that I dropped it, the runner's going to score.'

"And he kicked it right to the cutoff man at first base and he saved the run. He hit him right in the chest and the runner didn't score, they had to hold him up [on the single], and I think the Reds eventually won. It was a perfect kick!"

NEVER AGAIN!

In a 1996 game, Jose Valentin was playing shortstop for the Brewers when Oakland's Rafael Bournigal came to the plate with the bases loaded. Bournigal hit a blooper over the head of Jeff Cirillo, who was drawn in at third base. Valentin glided over, gloved the ball on a hop, and gunned to the plate for a force out.

That part of the play was routine, but after making the peg, Valentin covered third and took a return throw from the catcher to complete a wild 6-2-6 double play. "None of us will ever see that play again as long as we live," marveled Valentin.

WILD MAN

On May 24, 1995, Jason Grimsley was on the mound for the Cleveland Indians. Milwaukee's Kevin Seitzer reached first, then proceeded to take a tour around the bases thanks to three wild pitches. Over a hard-to-believe stretch of just six pitches, Grimsley uncorked the three errant throws. Further, it marked the second time that season that Grimsley somehow managed three wild pitches on just six throws.

DON'T NEED HELP

Later that same year, on September 11, the Yankees took on the Indians in a most unusual game. New York played the entire contest without recording a single assist. In the history of the game, such an oddity had happened a mere four times. The Yanks did it by chalking up eight outs on strikeouts, two by way of unassisted ground outs, and 17 fly balls, liners, or pop-ups.

NO HELP, PART II

Andy Van Slyke did something no outfielder had accomplished in almost 18 years when he recorded an unassisted double play on July 7, 1992. First he caught a fly ball for an out. Then he noticed the runner off first had taken off and had roamed way too far from his safe haven. Van Slyke casually trotted from center field to first base to complete the DP. He even had time to bounce the ball, like a deft NBA dribbler, off the artificial turf as he made his way to the infield.

WICKED WIND

The Texas-Detroit game of April 26, 1994, featured several weird plays due to 50 mph winds. Nature was so nasty that night, a streetlight near the ballpark at Arlington was uprooted. The craziness began when Jose Canseco of the Rangers lifted a pop-up into shallow center field. A few seconds later, Detroit's Cecil Fielder was startled when he saw the ball fall by his feet not far from first base. In the sixth inning, Rick Helling of the Rangers began his windup when a gust of wind blew him off the mound, bringing to mind the time Stu Miller committed a wind-induced balk at Candlestick during the 1961 All Star game.

NOW HITTING ...

Orel Hershiser's name was on the starting lineup card as the third baseman hitting in the number three slot during a game of September 15, 1993. While this was certainly odd, there was a logical reason behind this Dodgers move.

With Los Angeles on the road and batting first, manager Tommy Lasorda never even intended for Hershiser to hit. Instead, when it was Hershiser's turn to step up to the plate, Dave Hansen came off the bench to pinch hit. The move, it turned out, was merely a ploy to give Hansen, who stayed in the game as the third baseman after hitting, an official pinch at bat. He was in the process of trying to break the record for the most pinch hits in a season by a Dodger and his skipper was merely helping him out.

JUST PITCH TO HIM

Eric Plunk was on the hill for Cleveland with Lance Parrish behind the plate. The Minnesota Twins had the winning run at third with Kirby Puckett at bat. The Indians felt the situation called for an intentional walk, but regretted that decision moments later when Parrish couldn't handle one of the wide ones thrown from Plunk. The winning run scampered home on a rare play, but one that gave a solid argument against a suggested rule which would allow an intentional pass to be given without any pitches actually being made.

JUST LET HIM STEAL

On the first day of August 1992, Chicago Cubs outfielder Sammy Sosa managed to score all the way from first base on a steal despite the other team having executed, albeit poorly, a pitchout. He swiped second then continued on to third due to a wild throw that tailed off into center. Never hesitating around the third base bag, Sosa crossed home plate thanks, this time, to the nonchalant backup of the play by the center fielder.

LET 'EM REACH BASE, THEN ERASE THEM

The Toronto Blue Jays were visiting the Baltimore Orioles on August 24, 1983, when a strange inning took place. Baltimore's pitchers allowed a parade of opponents to reach base, but then methodically wiped them out. With Barry Bonnell on first base in the 10th inning, Tippy Martinez entered the game in a relief role with his O's down by a run. Martinez sensed Bonnell would try to steal since the Orioles had just replaced their catcher with a player who was normally an infielder, Lenn Sakata. Therefore, Martinez threw to first and was able to nab Bonnell.

The batter, Dave Collins, then drew a walk, only to be picked off by Martinez. Moments later baseball history was made when Willie Upshaw, who had reached first on an infield hit, was also picked off by Martinez. This was the first time in modern baseball that a pitcher was responsible for recording all three outs via pickoffs.

Ironically, Sakata, a defensive liability, indirectly led to the pickoffs. In addition, and more important, it was Sakata who won the game in the bottom of the 10th with a three-run shot.

LONGEST HOMER EVER?

On August 10, 2004, Reds outfielder Adam Dunn hit a home run that eventually traveled so far nobody could estimate its total distance. First of all, he smoked the pitch so hard it flew an estimated 535 feet on the fly, bounced on the street just outside of Great American Ball Park in Cincinnati, and finally came to rest on a piece of driftwood in the Ohio River. Fellow Reds outfielder Ken Griffey, Jr., feigning disbelief, muttered, "Someday I'll be that strong."

SELDOM SEEN

When Barry Bonds and Rafael Palmeiro both homered in the San Francisco Giants versus the Baltimore Orioles game of June 12, 2004, it marked only the third time two men with 500 or more homers connected in the same game. In fact, this feat had never taken place until 1970 when the incomparable Willie Mays of the Giants and Cubs great Ernie Banks both homered. Just a year later, as if it were about to become a commonplace occurrence, Mays and Atlanta slugger Hank Aaron both contributed home runs. Furthermore, had it not been for the existence of interleague play, Bonds and Palmeiro would not have met each other in the Giants game at Baltimore.

ANOTHER RARE HOME RUN FEAT

Jim Thome joined the Philadelphia Phillies in 2003 and achieved something only Ken Griffey, Jr. had ever done—his 47 home runs gave him back-to-back seasons of 40-plus homers in different leagues. Griffey's two years with 40 or more homers in both circuits came in 1999 with the American League Seattle Mariners and 2000 as a member of the Reds in the National League.

One reason such a feat is so rare is sluggers don't tend to get traded often (although with the advent of free agency, player mobility became more common and easier). Another factor lending to the difficulty of the feat is that when players move to a new league they must adjust to new conditions, mainly facing many new pitchers.

NUMBERS GAME

In a numerical oddity, Houston outfielder Lance Berkman, who was wearing his #17 jersey, hit his 17th home run of 2004 on July 17. Further research revealed an odds-defying fact—his last home run had come on June 17.

FIRST AND LAST ODDITY

Two obscure players made trivia history when they homered in their first and final big league at bats. Chicago Cubs catcher Paul Gillespie, who managed to play in only 89 games, did this in 1942 and 1945. In between, he hit only four additional home runs. John Miller, mostly a utility player, matched the feat when he broke in with the Yankees in 1966 and homered, then topped off his career by stroking a home run in his final big league appearance at the plate, doing that with the Los Angeles Dodgers in 1969. Noteworthy is the fact that those hits represented his only big league home runs and two of his paltry 10 lifetime hits over a 32-game career.

TRIPLE KILLING

Back on May 10, 1997, the Chicago Cubs turned a triple play due to the blustery conditions in the Windy City. It began when a pop-up was hit into shallow center field. Cub infielder Shawon Dunston went back for the ball and the umpires invoked the infield fly rule.

However, when Dunston fought the stiff breeze and lost the battle, the ball fell in. Although the batter is still automatically out in this situation, the runners off first and second were free to advance at their own risk. They tried but both failed, retired on what ended up as a zany triple play.

MISSED CHANCE FOR FAME

In 1991, Randy Ready had a chance to register an unassisted triple play for the Phillies, but for some reason elected not to do so. Here's what transpired: San Diego's Tony Gwynn ripped a line drive to Ready, who snagged it. He then stepped on second for an out on Paul Faries who had been running from second on the pitch. Then, even though Tony Fernandez was hung out to dry, having nearly reached second base (advancing from first on an ill-fated hit-and-run play), Ready tossed to first to complete the triple-killing instead of handling the third out on his own.

THREE WITH ONE STONE

On July 17 of 1990, the Twins did something that had never taken place in the majors: they turned two triple plays in one game. By way of comparison, the record for an entire season by a team is three.

Interestingly, both plays began with Boston batters hitting ground balls to Gary Gaetti at third base. In both instances he then fired the ball to Al Newman at second base and a relay throw on to Kent Hrbek at first resulted in third outs being recorded. Two odd items involving the game: A) the Red Sox won the contest anyway, 1–0. B) Sox skipper Joe Morgan commented on one of the plays in which he set the runners in motion, "Geez, I have them running to avoid the double play and we hit into a triple play."

NO-HIT MARVELS

On June 29, 1990, an oddity occurred when, for the first time ever, two no-hitters were thrown on the same day— one in each league. The first one came when Dave Stewart spun his beauty for the A's against the Blue Jays. A few hours later LA's Fernando Valenzuela repeated the feat versus the Cardinals.

The only other time two no-hitters took place on the same day had been eons ago with both no-hitters occurring in the same contest. In 1917 Jim "Hippo" Vaughn and Fred Toney matched up and threw what was labeled a double no-hitter.

A RAIN IN?

Everyone knows what a rainout is, but how about a rain in? Rex Hudler said the most astounding thing he ever saw over his lengthy stay in pro ball was "when I was playing in Montreal. They had the dome roof and they closed it one night and it rained. There were a couple of leaks in the roof, so bad they had to postpone the game. It was the first rainout ever in an indoor stadium—an indoor game postponed because of rain! "

STRANGE "RUN DOWN"

There's a tale that old-timers swear is true involving one of the most fantastic base running plays in the history of the game. It began when a runner crossed, but did not actually touch home plate. Thinking he had indeed scored, he headed into his dugout. The catcher, after being alerted of the runner's mistake, trotted over to the dugout as well. The story goes that since the catcher wasn't sure which player sitting on the pines was his true target, he commenced tagging everyone perched on the bench.

When he got near the actual at-risk runner, that player bolted toward home plate. It was too late, however, as the second baseman was covering the plate and the catcher threw the runner out.

OBSCURE DEFENSIVE "PLAY"

The last left-handed thrower to handle the catching chores in the majors was Pittsburg Pirates' Benny Distefano, who entered a game in the ninth inning on May 14, 1989. He recorded a putout on a strikeout and joined a very short list of lefty catchers. Of course, not being a star player, Distefano pointed out, "I'll do anything to get a chance to play." In all, he caught in three major league games while appearing in only 240 games overall, mainly at first or as a pinch-hitter.

As a matter of fact, after 1905 only two other left-handed throwers entered games as a catcher—Dale Long in 1958, twice as a member of the Chicago Cubs, and Mike Squires of the Chicago White Sox on two occasions in 1980. Incidentally, Squires also played third base 14 times, also unheard of for a left-handed thrower.

7
CAN YOU RECALL THE PLAY?

R*elive some famous plays and events from the past and accept the challenge of answering a question from each scenario.*

1. A REALLY LONG BALL

Fred McGriff has hit more than his share of homers and witnessed even more. Looking back through all the titanic blasts he's seen, the home run he felt was the most stupendous ever was one that was jacked completely out of Milwaukee County Stadium. "I thought that was incredible because that's a huge stadium," catcher Rick Dempsey recalled. "Dan Plesac threw a fastball and it just disappeared into the night." He was correct—it sailed some 30 feet above an eight-foot-high fence above the left-field seats and was the only fair ball to escape that park. Who hit it, and, within three years, when was this feat performed? Clues: The player was an enormously strong member of the Detroit Tigers who also played with Toronto, where he fizzled; Japan, where he blossomed enough to result in his return to the United States; and, later in his career, he also played for the Yankees, Angels, and Indians. Additionally, he once swatted 51 homers and is the father of a talented baseball player named Prince.

The answer is on page 84.

2. DRAMATIC ENDING

Reliever Mike Stanton was with the Atlanta Braves in 1992 when they won the National League pennant. His most unforgettable moment in the majors was when a teammate of his "scored on that ground ball in the hole [and into left field]. There's no way he should've scored as slow as [he] runs. And Barry Bonds comes up on the ball so fast [in the outfield], so good, but," he concluded in an announcer-like dramatic voice, "Braves go to the Series."

Braves catcher Javy Lopez added, "Francisco Cabrera got that base hit and I was in the bullpen. It was amazing that he got that hit to beat the Pirates." He was correct—Cabrera had very few moments of fame in the majors, lasting only 196 games and driving in just 62 runs, but baseball fans will forever remember his name. However, can you recall the gimpy player who managed to beat Bonds' throw to the plate to score the dramatic run? Clue: his initials are S.B. *The answer is on page 84.*

3. WHAT A SHOT!

During the 1989 American League Championship Series, a slugger for the Oakland A's teed off on a pitch and propelled it way up into the fifth level at Toronto's Skydome. Todd Hundley called that colossal shot, "The most amazing thing I ever saw. That was a bomb!" While other homers have traveled greater distances—Mark McGwire hit one further in the same park, for instance—this homer got off the bat so fast and soared so high during a vital game, it is still spoken of in hushed tones today. Who spanked that long drive? Clue: He was also the first man to steal 40 or more bases while hitting 40-plus homers in a season. *The answer is on page 84.*

4. WHAT A MISPLAY!

Not all memorable plays and events are positive ones. A Montreal Expos outfielder, normally a good one at that, once made the "Oops" blooper reels when he drifted into foul territory to haul in a Mike Piazza fly ball. Believing his catch was good for out number three, he handed the ball to a young fan in the first row of the stands and began to trot off the field.

Now, since there were actually only two men out, Los Angeles runner Jose Offerman alertly tagged up from first base. The outfielder, now realizing his folly, raced back to retrieve the ball. Eventually Offerman wound up at third base. Can you identify the fielder?

The answer is on page 84.

5. HELLO AND GOODBYE

In the sixth game of the 1947 World Series, this outfielder made a dazzling one-handed stab of a deep drive off the bat of Joe DiMaggio. It remains one of the most famous Series highlights ever. The outfielder lasted just four seasons in the majors and never gained much attention until his spotlight catch. Coincidentally, that defensive gem came in the final game of his career. Name this man.

The answer is on page 84.

6. INFAMOUS BLUNDER

The host Brooklyn Dodgers took a 4–3 lead into the ninth inning against the Yankees during Game 4 of the 1941 World Series when suddenly things began to go terribly wrong for them. Brooklyn relief pitcher Hugh Casey, needing just one out to tie the Series at two wins apiece, ran the count against Tommy Henrich to 3–2. What took place on the next pitch?

The answer is on page 85.

7. QUICKIE

What catcher was flattened by a steamroller named Pete Rose when the all-time hit king scored the winning run in the 1970 All-Star game? *The answer is on page 85.*

8. FUNNY, BUT YOU'RE STILL OUT

An amusing play took place when a future Hall of Famer, known for his power and certainly not for his speed, took off from first base on a hit-and-run play. When the batter swung through the pitch, the lumbering runner slid, but came up about six feet short of the second base bag. Coming up from his slide, and seeing the enemy shortstop was about to apply a tag, the dead duck runner smiled sheepishly at the umpire, formed a T with his hands, and called "Time out!" Needless to say, he was called out. Who was this all-time Pirate great? *The answer is on page 85.*

9. HE SHOULDA SLID

The scene was set: Game 5 of the 1968 Fall Classic between St. Louis and Detroit, with the Cards holding a commanding three-games-to-one lead. Cardinals ace Bob Gibson, with his phenomenal 1.12 ERA, had squared off twice against 31-game winner Denny McLain and had won both times, putting St. Louis in a pretty spot. Up by a run in the fifth inning, Cardinals speed merchant Lou Brock doubled, representing an insurance run. Julian Javier then singled to left where Willie Horton fielded the ball. Brock "nonchalanted" his way home, never sliding even though doing so could have resulted in a bang-bang play at the plate. He was tagged out.

Home plate ump Doug Harvey later mused, "He crossed home plate without touching it. He came in standing up. He should have slid."

Question: In the long run, did it matter or not—who won that Series? *The answer is on page 85.*

10. HUSTLE, OR ELSE

During a July 2005 contest between the New York Mets and the Florida Marlins, Carlos Beltran strode to the plate with a fellow Met on first. He proceeded to hit a popup to the Florida first sacker. Immediately recognizing his at-bat had been futile, Beltran disgustedly conceded the out and barely took a couple of steps towards first. Seeing this lack of hustle, the Florida first baseman purposely let the ball fall to the turf. He then picked it up and threw to second base for a force out and the front end of a double play. Can you recall who made this heads-up defensive play? Further, was it, in fact, so clever; is it legal to do what he did?

The answer is on page 85.

★ CHAPTER 7 ANSWERS ★

1. It was Cecil Fielder, and he did this in 1991.

★

2. Sid Bream.

★

3. Jose Canseco.

★

4. Larry Walker, winner of seven Gold Gloves. He later was able to shrug off his faux pas joking, "I get a lot of people asking me for balls now."

In a similar bonehead play from September 10, 1996, outfielder Derek Bell mistakenly lobbed a live ball into the stands. Clearly Bell thought the catch he made on a Marquis Grissom fly ball was the third out of the inning. A runner on first was awarded third on this miscue.

★

5. Al Gionfriddo.

6. Casey unloaded a dirt-low pitch (some say it was a "fast-breaking curve") that neither Henrich nor Dodger catcher Mickey Owen could handle. Although Henrich swung and missed for what should have been the game-ending strikeout, after the ball skittered by Owen, Henrich reached first safely. The floodgate opened and the Yanks thrived, rallying for four runs; the Dodgers never recovered, rolling over and dying in a five-game Series. Owen had committed only two passed balls that year, and many observers actually felt the blame belonged on Casey, contending that the pitch he had uncorked was actually a tough-to-handle spitball.

7. Cleveland Indians catcher Ray Fosse, in the bottom of the 12th inning. With two men out, Cincinnati's Rose singled and advanced to second on a base hit by Billy Grabarkewitz. Jim Hickman then singled, allowing the aggressive Rose to score when Amos Otis' throw from center field arrived a bit late to retire Rose at the plate.

8. Willie Stargell.

9. It mattered. From that point on, the Tigers stormed back and won it all in a seven-game set.

10. Carlos Delgado made the play. The play is legal. Delgado was very savvy on this play. Once in play the ball is, of course, live and since it fell to the field, the play is treated like a ground ball. When Beltran conceded an out at first, he failed to realize his lack of hustle would result in two outs, not merely one.

8
WHO HOLDS THE RECORD?

H *ow sharp are you when it comes to identifying baseball records?*

1. FAMOUS RECORD

Start with two easy ones dealing with legendary records. This all-time great never hit more than 12 home runs in a given month nor more than 47 in a season, yet his name is synonymous with power. *The answer is on page 91.*

2. ANOTHER FAMOUS RECORD

For sluggers, the 500 home run club is an exclusive group; to hit that many has been the equivalent of getting a free pass to the Hall of Fame. When it comes to pitchers, the 300 victory plateau is just as exclusive and magical. Name the only man with more than 500 wins. *The answer is on page 91.*

3. BASEBALL'S GREYHOUND

When this speed demon finally left the game, he was not only the record-holder for the most stolen bases in a season and a career, he also had scored more runs and, at that time, drawn more walks than any player ever. Then there was his record for the most lifetime leadoff homers and his even more awesome 3,000-plus hits. Name this man of many records. *The answer is on page 91.*

4. GOPHER BALLS GALORE

This pitcher holds the negative record for surrendering the most home runs in a single season, 50. However, when it came to a real killer of a curve, they should have labeled his nasty breaking ball "Deadman's Curve" because that lethal pitch put so many hitters away. Who is he?

The answer is on page 91.

5. MR DEPENDABLE

Through 2004, this pitcher has been the epitome of consistency, racking up 15 or more wins every season for 17 consecutive years. That eclipsed the former record held by the venerable Cy Young. Clue: The new record-holder has been with the Cubs twice, beginning his big league days there in 1986, and is a multiple winner of the Cy Young Award. *The answer is on page 92.*

6. A WHOLE LOT OF PRODUCTION

Ozzie Smith said the most impressive record that he witnessed was the "fascinating occurrence" when a St. Louis teammate hit a record-tying four home runs in a single game. Those homers also helped the player tie the record for the most runs driven in during a contest. Smith said that if his memory was correct, the player also walloped "the ball in the upper deck in Pittsburgh [Three River Stadium] all within a space of one week." Who is the man and how many RBI did he collect during his spree?

The answer is on page 92.

7. GERIATRIC CASE; ODD RECORD

In 2005, Pat Borders was salvaged from the scrap heap of disuse and old age in terms of baseball years. He was 42 when the Seattle Mariners signed him to a big league contract. During a game in May when the M's starting pitcher was also a 42-year-old, the two men made history as the oldest batterymates ever. Can you name this clever, soft-throwing hurler?   *The answer is on page 92.*

8. HOW TO PITCH TO MCGWIRE

When Mark McGwire was setting home run records for frequency and for distance in the 1990s, Florida manager Jim Leyland was asked how to pitch to the muscular 6' 5", 250-pounder. He quipped, "I have no idea. Roll it up there and hope it doesn't bounce?"

What player has since forced managers to use the intentional walk strategy more than any man ever?

The answer is on page 92.

9. MORE PRODUCTIVITY

Dave Winfield was with the Yankees when a teammate of his went berserk with the bat, setting a single season record for grand slams. Winfield remembered the player hitting "six grand slams in one year, all right in front of me, so I had a front row seat. He really cleared the bases; he had 24 RBI on six at bats!" Name the Yankee with the blistering bat.   *The answer is on page 93.*

10. BASEBALL'S METHUSELAH

Like Old Man River, this hitter just keeps on churning and rolling along. He turned 47 in August 2005, not long after he became the oldest player ever to steal a base. He also is the oldest ever to swat a pinch-hit homer, to play in 100 or more games, and to crush a grand slam. He has journeyed and played around the globe, appearing in 42 big league parks as well as stadiums in Japan, South Korea, Mexico, Puerto Rico, and the Dominican Republic. Who is this age-less wonder? *The answer is on page 93.*

11. BLAZING FAST

This man fired his pitches with the speed and explosiveness of an avalanche. When he retired in 1993, he owned just about every important strikeout record on the books; and, for the most part, he still is recognized as the King of K's. For example, while Randy Johnson has continued his string of strikeout pyrotechnics into the 2000s, this man's career strikeout record of 5,714 could stand for a very long time. Likewise, his seven no-hitters is a seemingly insurmountable record. Who is this fireballing phenom who struck out a record 383 men in 1973?

The answer is on page 93.

12. HIT 'EM WHERE THEY AIN'T

His 242 hits as a rookie in 2001 were more than anyone had amassed in 71 years. Then, in 2004, his 262 hits (good for a lofty .372 average) shattered the ancient mark for the most hits in a single season. Opposing managers simply hope he swats the ball right at somebody, or puts it high enough in the air that his outfield can run it down.

Rickey Henderson critiqued this man's style, noting, "[He] can use a turf field to his advantage, he uses more of a running-type start, a swing-type start, to get him [going] and then he places the ball. To me, he's sort of like a Tony Gwynn guy who can put the ball anywhere they want to; and they basically try to put the ball in the holes." Henderson drew another comparison. "He is a little faster than [Rod] Carew. Carew was more of the scientist as a hitter. He hits the ball wherever it's pitched."

Who is this outstanding record holder?

The answer is on page 93.

13. FIRST TO TOP RUTH

Lately every baseball fan is well aware that the 60 home run mark is not quite as mystical as it once was. Who was the first man to surpass Babe Ruth's single season record of 60 homers in 1927?

The answer is on page 93.

14. MONOPOLY ON THE CY YOUNG AWARD

Despite his age, this pitcher was still active and going strong as recently as 2005. Through 2004, he owned 328 wins, with a tiny 3.18 ERA, versus only 164 defeats, meaning he won two out of every three decisions he was part of. In postseason play, he has still managed to win big; 60 percent of his decisions are victories. In addition, he has captured more Cy Young Awards, seven, than any other pitcher in the history of baseball.

The answer is on page 93.

15. TOP BATTING AVERAGE

The last man to reach the .400 strata was Ted Williams when he laced the ball to a .406 tune in 1941. Impressive to be sure, but the highest average for a single season was a mind-boggling .424. What superstar was able to hit that high?

The answer is on page 93.

1. Hank Aaron, a man who lashed his bat with the speed and raw danger of Indiana Jones' bullwhip. Sparky Anderson praised Aaron's "fast hands and powerful wrists."

2. Cy Young, with 511 wins, ranks the number one of all-time. The nearest pitcher to him was Walter Johnson and he was almost 100 wins behind Young at 417.

Scott Rolen was in awe of Cy Young's record."Unbelievable the amount of wins that he had. I mean, that's the most amazing, I think, to me." Simple math reveals a pitcher who begins at as early of an age as, say, 19 could win 25 games every single season of his career through the age of 38 and he'd still be shy of Young's total.

Not only that, with today's five-man pitching rotations, winning 25 is nearly an impossible feat for any given single season, let alone for 20 years in a row. The last time a pitcher notched 25 or more wins was in 1990 when Bob Welch did it for the A's.

3. Rickey Henderson.

4. Bert Blyleven, winner of 279 games. As strange as it sounds, in 1986, the year he gave up his record 50 homers, he posted a fine 17–14 record. The following year, he generously issued an additional 46 homers to tie for the second most given up in a season.

5. Greg Maddux. Every year he is good for almost exactly 200 innings of toil and throughout his long, illustrious career he has spent only one stint on the disabled list.

6. Mark Whitten. He drove in 12 runs to tie the mark of Jim Bottomley. Interestingly, the man sometimes labeled "Hard Hittin' Mark Whitten" only hit 105 homers over 11 big league seasons. In all, only 11 men from the modern era have ever hit four homers during a nine-inning contest, including Lou Gehrig and Willie Mays.

The sensational Scott Rolen said of Whitten's home run outburst, "That's incredible, I don't know if it's chance or what it might be, but, I mean, that doesn't happen—it just doesn't happen! And 12 RBIs, that's a month right there in one game!"

7. Jamie Moyer. Borders, by the way, is also the answer to another trivia item: He is the only player ever to win the MVP of the World Series (in 1992 with the Toronto Blue Jays) and an Olympic gold medal (as a member of the 2000 Team USA).

8. Barry Bonds. In 2004, he drew an ungodly record-setting 232 bases on balls. By way of comparison, the most Ruth ever earned was 170, a stunning total before the Bonds era. Furthermore, 120 of Bonds' walks were intentional, yet another new record which far eclipsed marks set by previous record-holders (the American League record is a mere 33). Entering the 2005 season, Bonds had amassed 2,302 career walks (#1 all-time) leaving former record holders such as Rickey Henderson and Babe Ruth far behind.

9. It was popular first baseman Don Mattingly who powered six grand slams in 1987.

★

10. Julio Franco. In 2005, he was still playing baseball at an age older than 15 current general managers and eight field managers.

★

11. Nolan Ryan, also known as the Ryan Express, set the record for 383 strikeouts. Ryan's longevity was unmatched; he endured 27 years of violent deliveries to the plate, yet stayed remarkably healthy on route to his numerous records.

★

12. Seattle's Ichiro Suzuki, who also holds the record for the most singles in a season (225).

★

13. Roger Maris, who hit 61 HR in 1961, was the first man to top Ruth.

★

14. Roger Clemens.

★

15. Rogers Hornsby.

*B*aseball quotes are a big part of the game, so try your skill with these questions:

1. What Brooklyn Dodger pitcher once gave up a homer to Tommy Henrich that resulted in him losing a 1–0 heartbreaker? He somehow managed to keep his sense of humor when reporters asked him what pitch he had thrown to Henrich. The hurler replied, "A change of space." Clues: This Dodgers player posted a lifetime 149–90 record and his initials are D.N.   *The answer is on page 100.*

2. This man held numerous records for being hit by pitches. He'd often intentionally allow himself to get hit, at times resembling a walking bruise. He went so far as to purposely wear his uniform as baggy as possible, realizing that even if a pitch barely nicks an article of clothing, the batter is awarded first base. He summed up his philosophy like this: "Some people give their bodies to science, I give mine to baseball." Who was this scrappy man, who led the league in times hit by a pitch seven years in a row and a National League record 243 times over his career: A) Minnie Minoso; B) Don Baylor; C) Ron Hunt; or D) Frank Robinson?

The answer is on page 100.

3. This manager had the task of constructing the lineup of his highly talented American League All-Star crew. Armed with a plethora of power hitters, he finally settled on using RBI machine Manny Ramirez as his cleanup hitter.

A reporter asked a silly question about why Ramirez was hand-picked to bat fourth when other Dominican-born players were available. The manager joked, " We don't base the lineup on nationalities. If we did, I would have had an Italian." Who is this manager? *The answer is on page 100.*

4. The manager who guided the 2005 National League All-Star squad had this to say about one of his pitchers, John Smoltz. "I thought he was the best [closer] in our league [over the last few years]. Then he goes back to starting and is just remarkable." Smoltz made an appearance in the '05 mid-summer classic in Detroit, a fitting spot for the Michigan native whose grandfather was a member of the Tigers ground crew for close to 40 years. In addition, one of his uncles once had the job of placing numbers on the scoreboard at Tiger Stadium. Your job, however, is to identify the manager who left the 2005 game with a 3–1 record in All-Star play.

The answer is on page 100.

5. Just going on his physical appearance, it was hard to believe this player was as skilled as he was. He once won 25 contests and fanned 308 batters, yet he possessed a potbelly physique. A hard worker who once averaged 330 innings pitched over a four-year span, this man joked, "A guy will be watching me on TV and see that I don't look in any better shape than he is. 'Hey, Maude,' he'll holler. 'Get a load of this guy. And he's a 20-game winner.'" Was this pitcher: A) Rich Gossage; B) Mickey Lolich; or C) Wilbur Wood?

The answer is on page 100.

6. In 1989, Yankees general manager Bob Quinn announced they had re-signed one of their pitchers. Quinn intoned to the media, "I would not preclude [him] from appearing in different roles." He was, of course, saying the pitcher might wind up working as both a starter and a reliever. The player, however, quipped, "I'm not going to be playing the role of Hamlet, am I?" Who said it? Clues: This southpaw enjoyed one of the finest single seasons of pitching ever in 1978 when he went 25–3, fired nine shutouts, posted a microscopic ERA of 1.74, and won nearly 90 percent of all his decisions. *The answer is on page 100.*

7. This longball artist once said, only half-jokingly, "I don't break bats. I wear them out." Was it A) Babe Ruth; B) Jimmie Foxx; C) Josh Gibson; or D) Willie Stargell? *The answer is on page 100.*

8. One of this man's secrets to his hitting was he could foul off pitches, even hard-to-handle inside ones, so he was unafraid to hit with two strikes on him. One reason he was so comfortable with two strikes was summed up by George Brett who quipped, "A woman will be elected president before [he] is called out on strikes." What member of the 3,000 hit club and five-time batting champ was he referring to? *The answer is on page 100.*

9. One of the keys to Rod Carew's success was his uncanny bat control, which he employed in capturing seven batting titles over his first 12 years in the majors. Using a light bat, he'd smoothly guide the ball to any hole in the defense. In addition, as one of his managers once observed, with only slight exaggeration, "He could bunt .300 if he tried." Who came up with that quote? Clue: He was a fiery, even volatile, manager and is most remembered for his tumultuous days with the Yankees both as a player and manager. *The answer is on page 100.*

10. What all-time great was Rube Bressler of the Philadelphia Athletics speaking of when he said the man in question ". . . had that terrible fire, that unbelievable drive. He wasn't too well-liked, but he didn't care about that. He roomed alone." Bressler added, "I never saw anybody like him. It was his base. It was his game. Everything was his. The most feared man in the history of baseball."

The answer is on page 101.

11. This man had total confidence in his bat control, believing he could handle any pitch, in any location. "Pitch me outside," he once said, "I will hit .400. Pitch me inside, and you will not find the ball." Who was this four-time batting champ? *The answer is on page 101.*

12. In 1994, many fans felt this man would surely scorch 60-plus homers. He scoffed, telling the *Pittsburgh Post-Gazette* that sluggers such as Frank Thomas have "got those big pythons for arms. I've got little, skinny pythons. I can hit home runs, but I've got to get my whole little body behind it." What man, whose father also starred in the majors, was being rather modest as he later became a member of the 500 home run club?

The answer is on page 101.

13. Who is being quoted here? He began by saying people recalled him for his home run hitting, but also for his numerous strikeouts. "The strikeout is the ultimate failure and I struck out 1,936 times—more than any player but Reggie Jackson. But I'm proud of my strikeouts too, for I feel that to suceed, one must first fail; and the more you fail, the more you learn about succeeding." Was it: A) Babe Ruth; B) Mike Schmidt; C) Willie Stargell; or D) Willie McCovey?

The answer is on page 101.

14. Who was pitcher Bobby Shantz referring to when he said he had been warned about pitching to this all-time great? "It was great advice," he began, "very encouraging. They said he had no weakness, won't swing at a bad ball, has the best eyes in the business, and can kill you with one swing; he won't hit at anything bad, but don't give him anything good." Big clue: The man being discussed was nicknamed "The Splendid Splinter." *The answer is on page 101.*

15. What Hall of Fame center fielder once said that Babe Ruth "made a grave mistake when he gave up pitching. Working once a week, he might have lasted a long time and become a great star." Clue: His initials are T.S. *The answer is on page 101.*

16. What outfielder, who has played for St. Louis, Atlanta, Los Angeles, and Texas, as well as for the Atlanta Falcons in the National Football League, when asked to describe the difference between baseball's spring training and pro-football's training camp replied, "One word. Pain!" *The answer is on page 101.*

17. In 2001, Tampa Bay was a terrible team. While in the midst of a 14-game meat grinder of a schedule, playing the formidable Yankees and Red Sox, the Devil Rays manager commented, "We're not intimidated by anyone . . . because we've been beaten by everybody." Who uttered those words of despair and self-mocking humor? *The answer is on page 101.*

18. It was reported in an AP item that when this man was traded from the Phillies to the Angels he told Philadelphia manager Terry Francona that if he wound up facing his former team in the World Series he would "try to steal their signs," then confessed that that could present a problem for him because even when he was on the team, "I didn't know them." Clue: He was a powerful outfielder who, as a member of the Atlanta Braves, twice hit 30-plus homers while stealing more than 30 bases. His initials are RG. *The answer is on page 101.*

19. Tough one. In 1998, this Cincinnati catcher was astonished to discover the mammoth monetary demands Mike Piazza's agent had concocted when he negotiated a contract with Los Angeles. "I can't comprehend the money [said to be $100 million] Piazza is asking for. I can't comprehend the $80 million the Dodgers are offering. Heck, I can't comprehend what I'm making [$875,000]." Clues: The speaker was once traded for Kenny Lofton; his first name is Eddie—who is he?

The answer is on page 101.

20. In May 2004, Roger Clemens of the Houston Astros, during an off day, pitched against his son and a group of eight-year-olds in a "coach-pitch" league. When a teammate of the highly competitive Clemens learned this, he quipped, "Oh, yeah? How many did he knock down?" Clue: The speaker was a power hitting infielder.

The answer is on page 101

21. Sometimes restless players trying to "stay loose" will do almost anything to alleviate the boredom that sometimes sets in during a long season. In 2004, a Minnesota Twins designated hitter, perhaps inspired by reality shows such as "Fear Factor," took a dare from his teammates. For a pot of $550 he actually ate a live beetle. He later told a *St. Paul Pioneer-Press* writer, "Hey, I got a kid to feed." Ironically, what rather well-paid player made that comment?

The answer is on page 101

22. What all-time great, the consensus pick as the best leadoff man in the history of baseball, was pitcher Doc Medich talking about when he said, "He's like a little kid in a train station. You turn your back on him and he's gone."

The answer is on page 101.

1. Don Newcombe.

2. It was Ron Hunt who was willing to lean into the ball, even to the point of allowing himself to get plunked by a pitch in an Old-Timers Game! He held the all-time record for getting hit by pitches for quite some time. He said of ace pitchers who threw wicked fastballs, "If they throw too hard, I'll take one for the team. If you can't hit them, let them hit you."

Ironically, while beanballs never fazed him, "the only time I really got hurt was when Denver Lemaster hit my hamstring. I turned and tried to keep my balance."

3. Boston Red Sox skipper Terry Francona, obviously of Italian decent, made that observation.

4. The NL manager was Tony La Russa.

5. Mickey Lolich. He not only was a 20-game winner, in the 1968 World Series he came up big, winning a record-tying three games to guide his Tigers to the championship.

6. It was "Louisiana Lightning," Ron Guidry.

7. Josh Gibson. The standout from the Negro League was enormously strong and hit some still-talked-about tape measure shots during his career.

8. Wade Boggs.

9. Billy Martin.

10. Bressler referred to Ty Cobb, a fierce, obsessive player, to be sure.

★

11. Roberto Clemente, a great bad ball hitter.

★

12. Ken Griffey, Jr.

★

13. C. Willie Stargell.

★

14. Ted Williams.

★

15. Tris Speaker, who clearly made this statement shortly after Ruth made the switch to become a full-time outfielder, but well before Ruth went on a lifetime tear as a hitter.

★

16. Brian Jordan.

★

17. Hal McRae.

★

18. Ron Gant.

★

19. Eddie Taubensee.

★

20. Jeff Bagwell.

★

21. Matt LeCroy, perhaps with both beetle and tongue in cheek, made the comment about the $550.

★

22. Rickey Henderson.

10
NAME THAT YEAR

I n this chapter, a famous event is discussed. Your task is to guess from the multiple choice answers which year the event actually took place.

1. As mentioned earlier, one year Rogers Hornsby pounded the ball at an unfathomable .424 clip. They say records are doomed to be broken and men such as Cal Ripken, Jr. proved that seemingly unbreakable marks such as Lou Gehrig's string of 2,130 consecutive games played are not, in fact, untouchable. However, unless the game of baseball changes significantly, it's tough to imagine someone usurping Hornsby.

Then again, no man has reached the coveted, nice round number of .400 since Ted Williams did this in 1941, and even then, the man many consider to be the best pure hitter ever, fell 18 points shy of Hornsby's average. Since Williams, the game's greatest, such as Tony Gwynn (with a personal high of .394 in 1994), George Brett (.390 in 1980), Rod Carew (.388 in 1977), and Ichiro Suzuki (he hit as high as .387 in Japan and .372 in the American League) have flirted with but never attained the .400 level. How long ago did Hornsby hit his single season record high: A) 1920; B) 1924; C) 1925; or D) 1930?

The answer is on page 106.

2. Somewhat surprisingly, Tom Seaver gained a higher percentage of votes when he was elected to the Hall of Fame than any man who ever played baseball. He garnered 98.84 percent of all votes cast. This is not to diminish Seaver's status, but it is hard to imagine that he topped Nolan Ryan's 98.79 percent (second best), Ty Cobb's 98.23 percent (#3 all-time), and Hank Aaron's 97.83 percent (fifth best, one spot behind George Brett).

Now, remembering a player must wait five years (with rare exceptions) after he retires before he can gain admittance into the Hall of Fame, when did Seaver get voted in? Was it: A) 1990; B) 1992; C) 1996; or D) 2000?

The answer is on page 106.

3. Rickey Henderson, the greatest base burglar of alltime, set a single season record with 130 in 1982, a dozen more than previous record-holder Lou Brock had managed. However, one year Henderson also established the record for the most times being caught stealing in a season, 42 times. What year did this occur: A) 1978; B) 1980; C) 1982; or D) none of these?

The answer is on page 106.

4. One writer joked that there are 21, not the officially listed 20 members of the 500 home run club (through 2004). He explained the extra man is pitcher Robin Roberts, who dished up 505 gopher balls during his long and excellent (Hall of Fame-caliber) career. What year did he finish his career with that staggering record for homers surrendered: A) 1958; B) 1960; C) 1966; or D) 1968?   *The answer is on page 106.*

5. Bob Feller, also known as "Rapid Robert," once set a rather offbeat but certainly laudatory record when he, as a 17-year-old, struck out 17 batters. For years, no pitcher ever managed to fan the number of men that matched his age until Kerry Wood whiffed 20 while pitching for the Chicago Cubs at the age of 20. When did this monumental performance take place: A) 1996; B) 1998; C) 2000; or D) 2001?

The answer is on page 106.

6. For years the player who entered the 400 home run circle quicker than anyone was Babe Ruth. No too long ago that changed when Mark McGwire took only 4,726 at bats (128 fewer than Ruth) to hit his 400th homer. When did "Big Mac" accomplish this: A) 1996; B) 1997; C) 1998; or D) 2000? *The answer is on page 107.*

7. Doug Drabek posted a 12–11 record one year while being saddled with a sky-high 5.74 ERA. That marked the highest ERA for an American League pitcher with a winning record in the annals of the league. What year was that: A) 1992; B) 1995; C) 1996; or D) 1997? *The answer is on page 107.*

8. What year did Orel Hershiser of the Los Angeles Dodgers rack up his stellar streak of 59 consecutive scoreless innings: A) 1980; B) 1984; C) 1986; or D) 1988?

The answer is on page 107.

9. Norm Cash stung the ball at a .361 pace one year then plunged to a .243 average the following season. That marked the sharpest one-year decline ever among players who qualified for the batting crown. His .361 batting average did win the crown, but the following year was brutal. When did he suffer through his dismal fall off to .243: A) 1958; B) 1960; C) 1962; or D) 1964? *The answer is on page 107.*

10. In one of baseball's stranger "statistics," what year featured the coldest game-time temperature for the start of a World Series contest: A) 1994; B) 1995; C) 1997; or D) 1998? Clue: That game took place in Cleveland.

The answer is on page 107.

11. Fans thought Reggie Jackson was destined to eclipse Roger Maris' record for the most homers in a season when "Jax" got so hot he drilled 37 home runs by the All-Star break (four more than the previous record set by Maris by the '61 break). Guess which season Jackson set this unusual record: A) 1967; B) 1969; C) 1971; or D) 1974.
The answer is on page 107.

12. One year Brady Anderson saw his home run total fall from 50 the previous season down to a mere 18, said to be the largest one-year nosedive ever. That same season featured Nomar Garciaparra driving home 98 runs to set the record for the most RBI ever by a leadoff hitter. When did these two events take place: A) 1995; B) 1997; C) 2000; or D) 2001? *The answer is on page 108.*

13. Todd Helton was another post-Ted Williams hitter who came tantalizingly close to .400 one year. Playing for the Colorado Rockies in hitter-friendly Coors Field, he wound up hitting .372 to complement his 59 doubles, 42 HR and his gaudy 147 RBI. Name the year when Helton tore the cover off the ball: A) 1998; B) 2000; C) 2001; or D) 2002.
The answer is on page 108.

14. This year featured what many experts consider to be the most lopsided World Series ever. Further, and quite unexpectedly, the team that took a severe pounding through the first six contests wound up winning the championship. The offensive statistics were unbelievable: The losing team crushed the eventual champs 16–3 in Game 2, whitewashed them 10–0 in Game 3 while outhitting them 16–4, and shellacked them 12–0 in Game 6. For the entire Fall Classic, the losers outscored the winning team by better than a two-to-one ratio at 55 runs to 27, outhomered them 10–4, and outpitched them with a team ERA of 3.54 to a horrendous 7.11 ERA. When did this wild World Series take place: A) 1927; B) 1944; C) 1952; or D) 1960? *The answer is on page 108.*

15. Johnny Vander Meer, working in just his second big league season, fired a no-hitter on June 11 for the Cincinnati Reds, topping the Boston Bees. Incredibly, in his next outing four days later, he matched his excellence, no-hitting the Brooklyn Dodgers by a 6–0 margin. No man has ever again achieved back-to-back no-hitters. When did Vander Meer spin his magic: A) 1932; B) 1936; C) 1938; or D) 1940? *The answer is on page 108.*

1. B. Hornsby hit .424 in 1924.

2. B. Seaver became a Hall of Famer in 1992.

3. C. Henderson was gunned out 42 times the same year he stole his 130 bases, 1982.

★

4. C. Roberts served up his last round-tripper in 1966. The most he gave up in a season was an inflated 46 in 1956, then the all-time single season record.

★

5. B. Wood blew away a record-tying 20 Houston Astros on May 6, 1998, pitching a one-hitter in which he allowed no walks. Remarkably, he managed this in just his fifth big league start (upping his record to 3–2).

In his next outing, Wood smashed the old record for the most strikeouts over a two-game span when he K'ed 13 Arizona batters. His 33 combined strikeouts toppled the old mark of 32 shared by Nolan Ryan, Randy Johnson, Dwight Gooden, and Luis Tiant, putting the rookie Wood in mighty fine company.

As a coincidental tidbit, Wood, a Texan just like Ryan and Clemens, wears the same jersey number as those two strikeout artists, men he said inspired him. Wood also said he didn't have good stuff when he was warming up, but during the game "felt like I was playing catch."

6. C. McGwire hit his 400th homer on May 9, 1998.

7. D. Drabek's winning season with a steep ERA was in 1997. A National League pitcher, Guy Bush, went 15–10 for the Cubs in 1930 but registered an abysmal 6.20 ERA.

8. D. Hershiser's fabulous shutout streak took place in 1988, running from August 30 through his final start of the season, a 10-inning contest in which he shattered the old record. Over that span, he gave up just 30 hits while striking out 34 hitters.

9. C. Cash's off year was 1962. He went on to become a solid, but unspectacular .271 lifetime hitter over his 17-year big league career who never again sniffed a batting crown. His second highest average had been in 1960 when he hit a modest .286.

10. C. It was a bitter 38 degrees for the start of Game 4 of the 1997 World Series in Cleveland when the Indians hosted the Marlins from tropical Florida.

11. B. Jackson's torrid first half came in 1969; he finished the season with 47 homers, far off his earlier record pace.

12. B. Anderson's decline and Garciaparra's RBI record both took place in 1997.

13. B. Helton's sterling season mentioned was 2000.

14. D. The year of the lopsided World Series was 1960. The Pittsburgh Pirates prevailed over the mighty New York Yankees in seven contests, winning it all on Bill Mazeroski's ninth-inning, climactic home run.

15. C. Vander Meer's two masterpieces came in 1938, a year in which he went 15–10 overall.

11

ODD AND TRICK PLAYS

*S*ee if you can come up with answers and/or rulings on *some very strange plays.*

1. PITCHER DECEPTION

Pedro Martinez of the New York Mets is on the hill with enemy runners off first and third with, say, two outs. Martinez would like to get out of the inning the easy way, by picking off a runner rather than face the risk of offering up a juicy pitch to the batter. Is he permitted to fake a throw to third, swivel, and then fire the ball to first, perhaps catching a napping runner straying off the bag too far?

The answer is on page 113.

2. ODD INNING?

Is it possible for a team to lay down three sacrifice bunts in an inning? If so, has it ever happened in the major leagues?

The answer is on page 113.

3. ODD INNING, PART II?

Is it conceivable for a team to hit three sacrifice flies in an inning?*The answer is on page 114.*

4. GO FOR TWO

When Larry Rothschild was the Tampa Bay manager, he thought back to a trick play from his days in uniform with Cincinnati. His Reds took on the Giants under manager Roger Craig who "had a bunt play where, with first and second occupied, the third base man charged and the shortstop went to [cover] second base." Judging from the defensive setup mentioned, can you ascertain what the Giants were trying to pull off?   *The answer is on page 114.*

5. BILLY MARTIN TRICK PLAY

Longtime Braves coach Pat Corrales said, "Billy Martin had that bunt play when he had a left-handed hitter up. Rickey Henderson would take off stealing and the guy would bunt the ball to third base and Henderson wouldn't even think about stopping at second, he'd continue to third base." What name is given to such a play? *The answer is on page 115.*

6. SNEAK IN AND OUT

One tricky play that can work well at the amateur level goes like this: The shortstop works his way behind a runner off second base then breaks for the bag; the pitcher intentionally ignores the shortstop's pleas for a throw. Acting disgusted as if a sneak-in play had been blown, the fielder loops in front of the runner, making his way back to his shortstop position.

At that moment, hoping the runner is lulled into a sense of safety, the second basemen darts in behind the runner and this time a pickoff throw comes his way. Would such a play work in the big leagues?

The answer is on page 115.

7. MINOR LEAGUE SLEIGHT OF HAND

Roberto Alomar has run his share of trick plays, but there was one he saw in the minors which floored him. "It was around 1986," he began, "with somebody at first base and the pitcher threw the ball over there [on a pickoff move]. Then a guy who was on the bench rolled a ball out toward the outfield. The guy who was diving back to first base looked up; he saw the ball rolling away. The first baseman started going after that ball. When he did that, the runner started going to second [thinking the pickoff throw had been errantly fired into shallow right field]."

Once the runner began his dash, he was picked off easily, with the first baseman producing the "real" ball and making an easy lob for the out. Is this play legal?

The answer is on page 115.

8. AN OLDIE

Infielder Kevin Stocker recalled a play he thought was very creative from his days in the minor leagues. "When you had a guy on first base and a right-handed hitter was up, our catcher would catch the ball [on each pitch] and throw it back to the pitcher every time the same way [over and over and over]. Then, without even looking, he could come up and throw to first, but still be looking at the pitcher [as he had done on every throw earlier].

"The guy on first base often times would just think, 'Oh, he's throwing it back to the pitcher.' He'd lower his head and kind of walk to the base at the same time the ball got there and we'd tag him out." Other than the deception involved, what does it take on the catcher's part to make the play succeed? *The answer is on page 116.*

9. SQUEEZE

Which league tends to use the squeeze play more, the National or the American, and why?

The answer is on page 116.

10. KINGS OF TRICK PLAYS

Bobby Cox, through 2005 a four-time winner of the Manager of the Year Award, has cited two managers as creators of great trick plays. Do you know who they are: A) Danny Murtaugh; B) Billy Martin; C) Gene Mauch; D) Tony LaRusso; or E) Sparky Anderson?

The answer is on page 117.

11. EVERY LITTLE EDGE

Just for fun, let's say Boston's Johnny Damon is on third base and Yankees pitcher Mike Mussina is working out of the windup, paying little attention to Damon. Mark Bellhorn is the batter and, realizing the steal of home has been called for, he decides to slightly change his position in the batter's box. Where would he move that would give an oh-so-slight edge to Damon in his attempt to swipe home?

The answer is on page 118.

12. HANK SET HIM UP

Harry "The Hat" Walker managed Roberto Clemente and had many opportunities to see Hank Aaron in action, too. Walker said that Aaron was the better of the two players and that while Clemente was regarded as the better fielder, Aaron was underappreciated in that realm.

Walker then recalled that when Aaron was on the base paths he occasionally "baited Clemente." What deception did Aaron carry out on Clemente? *The answer is on page 118.*

13. YOU'RE THE OFFICIAL SCORER ONCE MORE

Texas Rangers reliever Scott Bailes entered the game against the Mariners who had two men out in the top of the ninth. He made two deliveries to Seattle's Rob Ducey, then picked Russ Davis off first base. The Rangers rallied in the bottom of the ninth inning to win it. Does Bailes get a win, a save, or neither? *The answer is on page 118.*

1. While pitchers can't fake a throw to an empty base or, for that matter, fake a throw to first (those moves would be called balks), what is described here is perfectly legal but very, very rarely works.

However, veteran pitcher Wilson Alvarez said he's not only seen it succeed, but he played with an expert at it when he was with the Chicago White Sox. "Oh, yeah," he smiled, "I saw that play many times with Jack McDowell. He used to pick off like four or five guys a year like that. I think he was the best in the league at that." He went so far as to say that this play works more often than one might expect at the major league level.

2. Yes, three sac bunts in an inning can happen and has occurred—14 times in all through July of 2005. The most recent took place on June 26th of 2005 when the Texas Rangers met their interstate rivals, the Houston Astros, in interleague play. Normally, every sacrifice bunt results in an out, so three in an inning seems impossible—the third out on a bunt would negate the scoring of that play as a sacrifice. However, in this instance, it was possible because Texas first baseman Mark Teixeira made a throwing error on one of the bunt plays so, naturally no out occurred there and the seventh inning wound up featuring three sac bunts!

3. Three sacrifice flies have been hit by one team in an inning. Here's the most recent time three sac flies were tagged in the majors—the first time ever in National League play.

Marlon Anderson of the Mets singled off the glove of Yankees first baseman Tino Martinez to start a wild second inning on June 24, 2005. Mike Mussina then issued a walk to David Wright and gave up a Doug Mientkiewicz bunt single down the third base line to load the bags. At that point, Ramon Castro's sac fly to Gary Sheffield in right tied the game 1–1 and allowed Wright to scamper to third. Jose Reyes followed with another sacrifice fly, which was also ruled an error when Bernie Williams misplayed the ball, taking his eyes off the ball then dropping it. So the run scored on the sacrifice, but the batter lived at first on the big E, and there was still only one out.

The record-setting fly came after Mussina's error on a pickoff attempt permitted Reyes and Mientkiewicz to advance to second and third. Mike Cameron completed the zany inning when he lofted a fly to Sheffield, allowing Mientkiewicz to score off a dazed Mussina.

4. Rothschild said if the team bunted the ball to third, and most teams tried to do just that, a hard-charging third baseman would seize the ball "and they'd throw to second base to try to [start] the double play to get out of an inning. It was an unusual play and it worked a couple of times." Getting the lead man at second wasn't too tough, but they'd succeed in turning a twin killing if they employed the play under ideal circumstances. For example, said Rothschild, "We had a slow runner, Joe Oliver, [at the plate] which you have to have to try to get a double play there. It was the first time we'd seen the play and it happened twice in a series and it worked both times."

5. Corrales said it was basically a bunt and run and "instead of one base [on the bunt], they'd get two bases." Corrales, by the way, said that the Braves don't go for tricks as a rule, realizing they can often backfire on a team. Half-jokingly he said the best "trick is not to let the guy get to first base."

6. Wilson Alvarez offered his mixed opinion: "At this level, whatever it takes. It might work, but we [really] don't use it." In other words, he seems to think it never hurts to try some sleight of hand, but felt this particular one seems better suited for much lower levels of play.

Nevertheless, Baltimore's Cy Young Award winner Mike Flanagan said his team actually used to run similar plays. "At second base we used a combination pickoff [much like the play described above] with the second baseman and shortstop. The second baseman would go [to the bag to take the first pickoff throw]. Then, as soon as that play ended, the second baseman would start leaving; then the shortstop would come in behind—that was a little bit different." The play hinged on the fact that as soon as the runner began to once more "take his lead, then our shortstop would come in" and trap the complacent runner on the second throw.

The Orioles, under legendary skipper Earl Weaver, attempted, said Flanagan, "a lot of different pickoff plays. We'd also put the first baseman behind the runner [at first] and have a timing play [with the fielder sneaking in at first to take the pitcher's pickoff throw]."

7. No, but believe it or not, Alomar recalls the defense "got away with it."

8. According to Stocker, "It takes a good arm from the catcher to be able to come up and just kind of flick it toward first [in the manner of his other throws]. The idea is not to come up and fire it. The idea is to keep the same motion and just kind of flick it. The rhythm has got to be the same. Of course, the first baseman's gotta be ready, too. It's not really a set play, it takes everyone being alert." Everyone, that is, except the runner who "you can kinda get him sleeping."

★

9. Neither league uses this trick play as much as they used to in, say, the dead ball era, but, Wilson Alvarez commented, "They don't use it a lot in the American League. Once, maybe twice a year; they always play for the big innings." One reason the "Junior Circuit" doesn't tend to play for a run here and a run there is they employ a designated hitter. So, with one additional strong stick in their lineup, they shy away from giving away outs which takes place on most squeeze plays. Instead, they send their heavy artillery to the plate and take their chances on scoring runs in bulk.

One manager disagreed somewhat. Larry Rothschild said he ran the play with the Devil Rays. "It depends on your team and if you have the right elements in place. Good plays are made by players being able to perform different things. If the squeeze is going to put you ahead going into the ninth inning, you take your chance with it. If that means you're going to get the lead by squeezing, then you take the chance and do it. Any way you can get ahead, you take advantage of it.

"You have to have the right situation to do it. If you feel it's your best chance to score that run whether you're not comfortable with the hitter hitting a sac fly or where the infield is [playing] with the runner on third [you do it]. Whatever the elements might be dictates that you say, 'My best way to score right here is the squeeze.' The only thing you worry about is if they're going to pitch out because they know it's your best chance, too."

Many managers feel that nowadays even relatively light hitters have bulked up so there's a better chance a player can at least hoist the ball deep enough to the outfield to score a run on a sacrifice fly than lay down a decent bunt. Remember, if a batter, even one who's a superb bunter, gets a poor pitch to handle, the runner barreling down from third is trapped in no man's land for an easy out. The offense worked hard to get the man to third, so why take a gamble that could erase him from the base paths?

10. C and E. Bobby Cox believes, "Gene Mauch and Sparky Anderson gave a lot of thought into strategy and things like that. I can just tell you I learned a lot from just watching those guys do little things. Those guys originated all that stuff, to me. I thought Roger Craig was pretty much of an innovator himself. Of course, he was with Sparky a long time. Those types of guys would surprise you with stuff; you had to be on your toes."

As for their unusual ploys, Cox said, "I like that type of stuff; why not try it?" He said managers shouldn't merely go by the book and make the obvious managerial moves "when you think something else should work." Plus, he added that trying trick plays is a lot of fun at times.

He even felt "the hidden ball trick is always a good one" and should be attempted once in awhile, labeling former Yankees shortstop Gene Michael "the master at that— he was the best." More recently, Spike Owen and Matt Williams succeeded in duping runners on the ancient play.

11. While Bellhorn can't interfere with the catcher, Bobby Cox explained what Bellhorn should do: "The batter should get as deep in the box as he can to force the catcher back in order to [make it harder for him] to make a tag. I'm sure Mauch's the one who thought of that, him or Sparky."

It helps, too, for the batter to be a righty since he'd be standing on the third base side of the plate, meaning his body would obscure the catcher's vision of the runner bolting down the line.

12. After Clemente had fielded a ball, perhaps on a ball Aaron hit for an apparent double, "Aaron," recalled Walker, " would run into second base like he was going to break his stride [slowing down to settle in at second] and Roberto would start to throw [the ball softly back to the infield]. Then, thinking Aaron wouldn't go, he'd drop his head. Then, boom, Aaron would take off to third base." In effect, Aaron, on offense, had deked Clemente into relaxing, then took an extra base on him.

Deception is a big part of baseball. Just ask a batter who was geared up for a fastball then whiffed on a pitch delivered at glacier-like speed. As Walker pointed out, Aaron's trick led to a risk-free extra base for the Braves.

13. Every time a defensive player touches the ball, that portion of the play must be accounted for. The ruling is 3 [representing the first baseman] to 4 [Giles, in this case] and on to 1 [Davies recording the putout]. LaRoche even gets credit for an assist on the play, as does Giles, of course.

12
LAST CHANCE TO PLAY MANAGER

Your test of big league baseball knowledge began with managerial decisions. Now, to wrap things up, here's a final chance to do additional role playing with you as the manager or coach.

1. GREEN LIGHT?

It was the Cubs' Opening Day of 2000, and runners were on first and third with two outs and Sammy Sosa at the plate in the eighth inning. St. Louis led 7–1 when Eric Young began inching off first base, either to get a good two-out jump or possibly to swipe second.

Cardinals pitcher, right-hander Mark Thompson, pulled the old "fake a throw to third then whirl and fire the ball to first" move. And, even though it usually succeeds only in drawing derisive crowd reactions, this time it worked. Young was nailed. Why was this an utterly foolish move on Young's part and a big blow to the Cubs' chances?

The answer is on page 122.

2. PITCH COUNT MANIA

You are the Chicago Cubs manager Dusty Baker and the year is 2004. Your most pressing issue now may well be the critics who say you are using All-Star pitcher Carlos Zambrano too much. In today's game pitch counts are kept religiously and studied the same way.

Now, the 23-year-old Zambrano is a pretty big guy at 6'5" and 255 pounds, and he has said he could throw as many as 150 pitches in a game if called upon to do so. By early July he had gone over the 120-pitch mark in four of his last five starts. Do you, as his manager, start to back off now as the summer heats up?

The answer is on page 122.

3. MORE ROLE PLAY

Imagine you are Dusty Baker of 2004 once more, but this time you have to deal with the ego of your star slugger Sammy Sosa. Lamentably, Sosa is in the middle of a 13-game slump, hitting a meager .157 over that period. Not long ago you told the media that you were afraid of moving him lower in the batting order—he hadn't hit lower than the cleanup slot since July 8, 1994—because that move might lead to losing Sosa "psychologically or spiritually." Now, for the good of the club, you feel you must shove him down to the number five spot in the lineup. After all, of the 52 men who have hit cleanup with 100 or more at bats this season, Sosa's .220 batting average was the weakest. How do you break the news to him? In the days of "old school" baseball you might simply let him see his name on the lineup card and figure things out on his own; is that type of managing passe now?

The answer is on page 122.

4. SEPTEMBER CALLUPS

The year was 1973 and Oakland manager Dick Williams' roster was ripe. Due to the rule that allows teams to expand their rosters from the normal limit of 25 players come September 1, Williams had an abundance of second basemen, none known for their hitting skills, on the team. In the thick of a pennant race, Williams came up with a solution to his batting order's weak spot when his second baseman was due at the plate.

Did he: A) stick with the second sacker with the (relatively) hottest hand at the time; B) rotate a new second baseman into the lineup each night; or C) replace a second baseman by using a pinch hitter then plugging in a new man in the field every time one of his weak sticks had a turn at the plate?

The answer is on page 123.

5. FINAL CALL

In this scenario, you are manager Mike Hargrove of the Cleveland Indians. You have called upon your bench for a pinch hitter to replace star third baseman Travis Fryman in what would have been his last at bat in Tiger Stadium (as it was soon replaced by Comerica Park). Fryman, a former Tiger who hit right-handed, would have loved the opportunity to say farewell to his old ballpark and the Detriot fans who still appreciated what he had done in a Tigers uniform. The highly upset Fryman fumed on the bench, but Hargrove didn't notice as he was simply making the move he felt would best benefit the Indians, using a left-handed pinch hitter to face a Detroit righty.

Now, the next day Hargrove learned from his coaches about Fryman's ire. What would you do in Hargrove's situation? Keep in mind, Fryman had the reputation as a consummate team player, very unselfish.

The answer is on page 123.

6. TO GO OR NOT TO GO

In May 2002, Cleveland's Omar Vizquel led off third base and Matt Lawton was on first with the Indians leading Baltimore, 4–1. With two men out and Travis Fryman at the plate facing Orioles pitcher Sean Douglass, who was working out of the stretch position, Vizquel took off for home on a straight steal. Is this play wise, unconventional?

The answer is on page 123.

7. RUNNING WILD

Would you consider employing a triple steal—setting all three runners in motion with the bases loaded? After all, even if the lead runner is out at the plate, you'd still have two men in scoring position, or is this play way too dicey?

The answer is on page 124.

★ CHAPTER 12 ANSWERS ★

1. What's the advantage of Eric Young stealing? Down by six runs, a stolen base would be meaningless, hardly worth the chance of getting caught stealing or, worse, picked off. If he wasn't thinking of stealing, then straying too far off base was absolutely ludicrous. Additionally, by making the third out of the inning, he took the bat out of Sosa's hands in a situation where a home run could have drawn the Cubs closer to the Cards.

2. Baker observed that the critics were "not questioning" the pitch count on Carlos, "they're questioning the pitch count on me. People go way overboard with this pitch count. What happened before the pitch count? It just gives something else for people to write about or talk about. And it gives them something else to second-guess and ridicule the manager about." Still, pitchers' arms are highly valuable commodities and, as such, must be protected.

3. Nowadays not even hard-line managers would treat a star in "old school" fashion. Baker called Sosa into his office and suggested the move. Baker announced that Sosa indicated that "it would be better for the team and the way he's going to drop him down in the order . . . He said he wanted to do what was best for the team to help us get to the playoffs and to the World Series." Players of Sosa's standing do get special treatment, and do get coddled. The short-term results of the switch were positive with Sosa homering in two of his next three games. Long range, it didn't matter as the Cubs did not make post season play and Sosa and the Cubs became alienated—he moved on to become a member of the 2005 Baltimore Orioles.

By the way, in the first game after the 2005 All-Star game

Sosa, hitting just .225, was moved out of his customary five hole in the lineup. Manager Lee Mazzilli actually inserted Sosa into the second slot in his order, of all places. Sosa went 0–for–4 with a sac fly while striking out three times.

4. C. In a clever and unique move, for the season's final three weeks, Williams used four second basemen every game. By the way, his A's wound up winning the pennant.

5. You should (and Hargrove did) salvage Fryman's sore ego. Hargrove, also a class act, called Fryman in, explained what his thought process had been, and apologized to his third baseman. Fryman accepted the mea culpa and it was reported that the rest of the Indians, who were sympathetic to their buddy Fryman, appreciated Hargrove's actions.

6. Don't blame the manager in this instance. First of all, Vizquel went on his own so Fryman might have been swinging away, perhaps even injuring Vizquel. Fryman later commented, "I saw Omar out of the corner of my eye . . . It did catch me off guard, though." He added, "Normally you only try it when the pitcher is using the windup. I guess it's a good play if you make it."

Cleveland manager Charlie Manuel commented, "I had no problem with it. Why not do it there? Give the other team something to think about. When I managed in the minor leagues, we would always run all of our plays the first time through the league just to show the other teams everything we had so they had something to think about the rest of the season." Therefore, it was probably not a very smart baseball move, but a bold one to be sure.

7. While rare, pulling off a triple steal certainly has been done. In one case, Minnesota's Rod Carew was on third, Tony Oliva led off second, and Harmon Killebrew was nestled in at first. All three took off against Seattle pitcher Bucky Brandon, and all three made it. By the way, Carew's steal was one of a record-tying seven times he pilfered home (out of eight attempts) in 1969. The Twins under manager Billy Martin pulled off another triple steal with Carew as the lead runner later that year.

That season Martin loved his base runners to scoot freely. He had them burgle five bases in a matter of a few pitches on May 18, 1969. The onslaught began when Cesar Tovar stole third. Then, after Carew drew a walk, Tovar pulled off a double steal with him. Shortly after that, Carew stole third and home.

ABOUT THE AUTHOR

Wayne Stewart was born and raised in Donora, Pennsylvania, a town that has produced several big league baseball players, including Stan Musial and the father-son Griffeys. Stewart now lives in Lorain, Ohio, and is married to Nancy (Panich) Stewart. They have two sons, Sean and Scott.

Wayne has covered the sports world as a writer for over 25 years now, beginning in 1978. He has interviewed and profiled many stars including Kareem Abdul-Jabbar, Larry Bird, Lenny Wilkens, and baseball's legends such as Nolan Ryan, Bob Gibson, Tony Gwynn, Greg Maddux, Rickey Henderson, and Ken Griffey, Jr.

Wayne has written 18 baseball books to date, including *Baseball Oddities, Baseball Bafflers, Baseball Puzzlers, Indians on the Game, Fathers, Sons,* and *Baseball, Hitting Secrets of the Pros,* and *Pitching Secrets of the Pros,* along with 10 juvenile baseball books featuring the history of big league franchises. Some of his works have also appeared in several baseball anthologies.

Wayne has also wrote written nearly 700 articles for publications such as *Baseball Digest, USA Today/Baseball Weekly, Boys' Life,* and *Beckett Publications* (football, baseball, and basketball). In addition, he has written for many major league official team publications such as those for the Braves, Yankees, White Sox, Orioles, Padres, Twins, Phillies, Red Sox, A's, and Dodgers. Stewart He appeared, as a baseball expert/historian, on Cleveland's Fox 8 and on an ESPN Classic television show on Bob Feller. He also hosted his own radio shows on a small station in Lorain—a call-in, sports talk show; a pre-game Indians report; pre-game Notre Dame shows; and broadcasts of local baseball contests.

INDEX

SOURCES OF INFORMATION

Most of the quotes which appear in this book come from interviews the author conducted with players, coaches, and managers. Additional sources of information are listed below.

Books:
Baseball's Best Managers, by Harold Rosenthal
Baseball's Greatest Players, by *The Sporting News*
Baseball Quotations, by David H. Nathan
Umpires, by John C. Skipper

Periodicals:
Baseball Digest
Major League Baseball newsletter
SABR newsletter

Newspapers:
Associated Press and wire services
Elyria Chronicle-Telegram
The Morning Journal
Philadelphia Inquirer
The Plain Dealer
St. Paul Pioneer-Press